Lake District - North

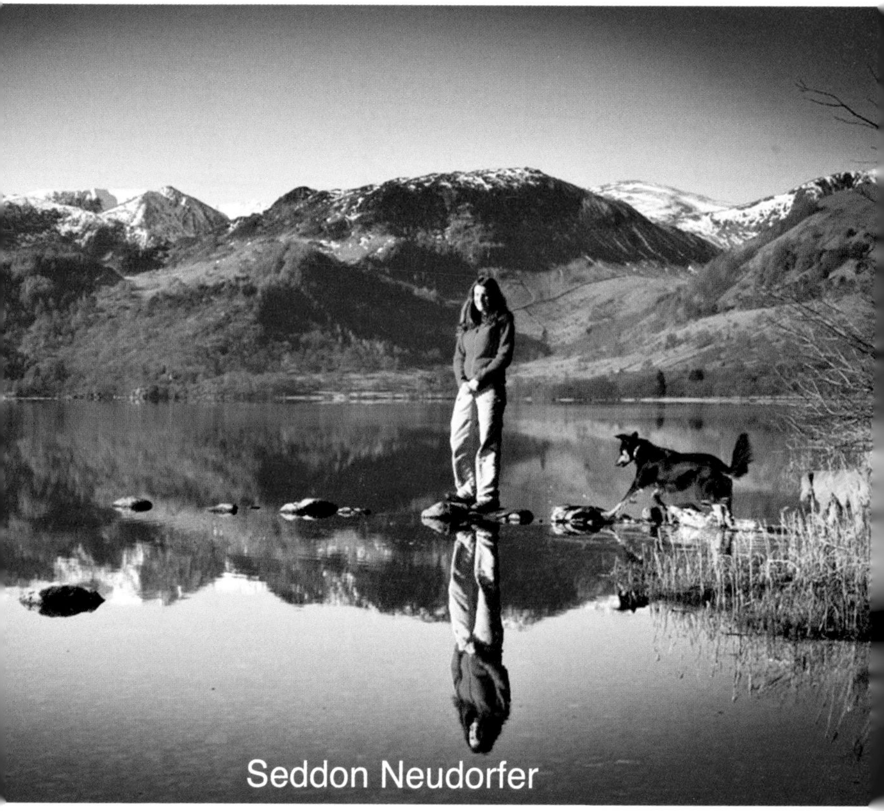

Seddon Neudorfer

www.countrysidedogwalks.co.uk

First published in July 2013 by **Wet Nose Publishing Ltd**
Reprinted August 2015
Summer Roost
Graigfechan
Denbighshire
LL15 2EU

All enquiries regarding sales telephone: 01824 704398
email cdw@wetnosepublishing.co.uk
www.countrysidedogwalks.co.uk

ISBN 978-0-9573722-3-8

We would like to dedicate this edition to James (pictured pg 54 with his much loved dog Sammy) who sadly lost his life so young.

With a special thank you to: Daisy Gibbs, Michael and Sheila Curtis, Alex Cameron, Mark and Jill Parry, Lorraine and Gerald Smith, Elaine and Neil Cox, (Peter, Chris, Karen and Frazer at **Podgy Paws Pet Shop** in Keswick).

 British Library Cataloguing-in-publication data.
A catalogue is available for this book from the British Library.
Printed in Poland by LF Book Services

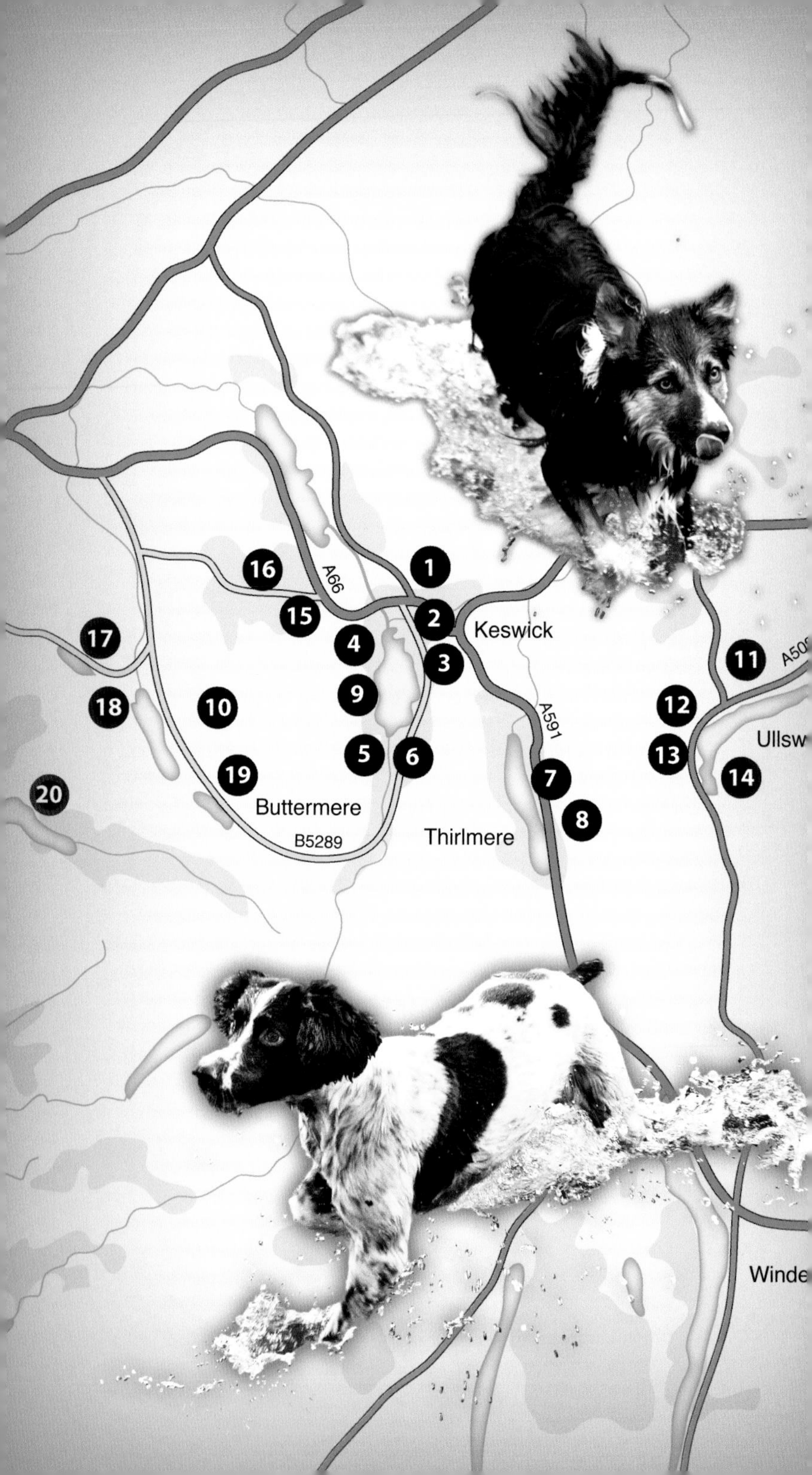

1
2
Keswick
3
4
9
15
16
A66
17
18
10
5
6
19
Buttermere
B5289
20
A591
7
8
Thirlmere
11
12
13
14

ontents

Check page 38 for advice regarding mountainous terrain.

Introduction

The twenty walks included in this book are all designed so that you and your wet nosed friend have a really enjoyable time. Where there are stiles, they are specially designed with lift gates for dogs. At a quick glance there is information at the beginning of each walk to tell you what to expect and what you may need to take with you. The descriptive guides will also warn of any roads ahead or areas of livestock so that you can get your dog on the lead well in advance.

Dogs just love to explore new places. They really enjoy the new smells and carry themselves a little higher with the added excitement. Going to new places gets you and your dog out and about, meeting new people and their dogs. It is important to socialise dogs, as they will be more likely to act in a friendly manner towards other dogs as they gain confidence.

The stunning pictures in this book are just a taster of what you can see along the way. Most of the walks are crammed with fantastic views and you are never far from water or woodlands: the latter will provide shade in the summer and shelter on cold, wet days where your dog will love the freedom to run up and down.

The walks are graded Easy, Medium and Challenging. They are all around one to three hours long, depending on your and your dog's pace. You may start with the easy ones and work up to the challenging walks depending on your and your dog's fitness. Different dog breeds and dog age must be taken into account when you decide which walks to do.

Different breeds of dog have different levels of fitness. For example, bulldogs can only do short walks whereas a border collie or a springer spaniel are extremely energetic and difficult to tire out. It is recommended that you do some research on the breed of dog that you own to get to know what sort of exercise that they require.

You may have a walk that you are happy doing with your dog every day, but this book will show you new areas to explore with a change of scenery and

a chance to meet new people and their dogs. Dogs love new places to visit and you will see the change in them as they explore the new surroundings, taking in the new smells with delight. You will fulfil both your life and your dog's just by trying somewhere new.

The Whinlatter and Knott Head walks are forested, where your dog can enjoy the freedom to run up and down without you having to worry about livestock. They are great for hot days, as many dogs don't cope well in the sun. There is plenty of water for your dog to enjoy, whether it be lakes, tarns, rivers or streams, so for those dogs that love water you can be sure they won't stay dry for long.

Some of the walks include bridleways, so you may encounter horses. It is important to put your dog on a lead if you see horses approach. It is always helpful to say hello to the riders as they near so that the horse realises that you are not a threat.

The Lake District National Park

The Lake District National Park was formed in 1951 to protect the beauty of the mountainous landscape and tranquil lakes from being developed into housing and industry. Most of the National Park is owned privately. Roughly 25% belongs to the National Trust and 3.9% belongs to the Lake District National Park Authority.

The villages and farmland only add to the beauty, complementing the natural landscape with its heathlands, hedgerows, beautifully crafted stone walls that are blanketed in moss, and the quaint cottages and beautiful houses that have been built from local stone.

Forests

On rare occasions the Forestry Commission may temporarily close paths due to forest works but again this is even less likely on a weekend. Any changes to the path networks that may occur after the date of print will be updated on our website.

Ground Nesting Birds

During 1st March through to end of July there will be several species of birds that make their nest on the ground. Dogs can disturb or harm chicks if they roam amongst the heather and bracken. During this time it is essential to keep your dog on the paths whilst walking amongst the heathland and grassland areas. Birds in the United Kingdom are split into three categories of conservation importance - Red, Amber and Green. Red being the highest conservation priority, with species needing urgent action. Amber is the next most critical on the list followed by green. For more information on this please see the BTO or RSPB websites. Birds that will be breeding on the Red data list include Sky lark, Twite and Hen harriers. Birds on the Amber list include Curlew, Snipe and Meadow pipits.

Rivers

Some dogs love water and will think nothing of plunging into the river. With the extreme weather conditions over the last few years, a river that may be safe for your dog to swim in can change in a matter of hours to become a swollen torrent that could wash your dog away. Please be careful when near rivers if there have been heavy periods of rain or if they look swollen or fast flowing. It is best to put your dogs on the lead, until you have assessed the situation.

Ticks

If you have been walking in areas where sheep graze you should check your dog for ticks. They must be removed as soon as possible. It is best to use tick tweezers, which are specially designed to remove the head and leg parts of the tick. Ticks can carry diseases and the longer they remain latched on to your dog the more the chance of spreading infections.

ivestock
ll walks avoid areas that cattle and horses graze. This can change however, ccording to changes of farming with the individual landowner. If you find that ɔu need to cross a field with cattle or horses and they seem interested in you ˙ your dog it is recommended within the Countryside Code to let your dog off e lead. Never try to get between livestock and your dog. Your dog will get ıt of a situation a lot more easily with speed than you can. It is usually only ıttle with young calves that are a threat, or young heifers or bullocks that nd to get a little inquisitive. They will usually stop when they get close to you ˙ your dog.

ost horses will come over for a fuss but a small proportion do have a oblem with dogs. They may see them as a threat and will act to defend the ɪrd. Horses that are out with a rider are completely different as they are not ɪfending the herd, and as long as you keep a safe distance there should not ɪ a problem. Sheep are not a danger to you, but your dog can be a danger them. Where sheep are grazing it is vital that you have your dog on a lead under very close control. You will know your dog, but if you are unsure it is tter to play safe and keep your dog on a lead. It is important always to have ur dog on a lead when around lambs. Lambs have a higher pitched bleat d are about the size of a cat, and your dog may act differently amongst ɪm.

ɒes Your Dog Fetch a Stick?
ɒst dogs love sticks and will pick them up without any encouragement from ɪir owners. Vets and dog trainers recommend that you should not throw ɔks for dogs. They can cause nasty injuries, sometimes fatal as the stick ı pierce the throat, or rebound off the ground and cause harm to your dog.

ɪg Fouling
ɪase be a responsible dog owner and ensure that you pick up after your g and place the dog bag in the bins provided. In the event that there are no s please take the dog bag away with you to the nearest road-side bin. The ˙estry Commission have a stick and flick policy so there is no need to pick ɒ, just flick it off the paths leaving it to degrade naturally. This is far better ın leaving non-biodegradable bags on the ground, which looks unsightly ɪ can stay there for months, maybe years.

1. Latrigg

Easy - 2 miles -

This is a super walk, which gives totally amazing views over Keswick and th surrounding area, including Derwent Water and Bassenthwaite Lake. The views are achieved with very little effort, as the car park is high up in the hills There are no roads but there may be sheep grazing.

How to get there – From Keswick take the A591 signed for Carlisle. After the first roundabout once on the A591 take the first right hand turn and follo signs for Skiddaw. You will reach the car park at the end of the narrow road.

Grid Ref – NY280253 Nearest
Post Code – CA12 4PH

Parking – Free car park but best to get there early as limited spaces.

Facilities – There are no facilities.

You will need – Leads, dog bags and water for your dog.

The Walk

❶ From the far end of the car park go through the pedestrian gate. Turn right through another gate, then left onto the gravel path, which veers right. You will instantly have stunning views of the hills to your right and behind. Following the path as it gradually ascends, you will be met with breathtakingly beautiful scenes across to the mountain ranges and below to Keswick. The town has a lake at each end: Derwent Water to your left and Bassenthwaite Lake to your right.

The path then takes a sharp left turn. Ignore a path on the right and continue to climb a little higher, still with the views on your right. ❷ You will pass a bench on the right where you can sit a while to soak up the atmosphere. As you continue you will have new views ahead of the rolling hills, passing a plantation on your right and some pine trees near to the path. Go through a gate and follow the worn grassy path, continuing straight ahead.

A little further along you will find yourself on the edge of a hill, passing patches of gorse on the slope of the hillside for a short distance. Go through the middle of the field as the slope weaves off to the right. As you see the fence line ahead of you, look out for a path that veers off to the left. ❸ Take this path but don't go through the farm gate ahead - instead turn left and proceed along the track.

Stay with the fence line and mixed woodland to your right. The track will bend sharply to the right. Pass through a gate at the stile straight ahead of you. Leaving the trees behind now, stay on the gravel path cutting through the hillside. You will soon see the car park ahead.

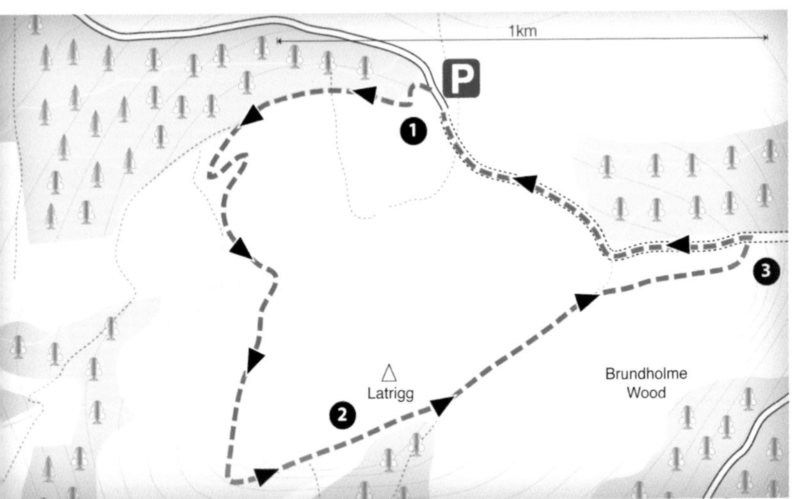

2. Latrigg - Brundholme Woods Chall - 4 miles - 2hrs

This is a great walk and very handy from the town of Keswick, beginning and ending at Fitz Park. It is largely liner, with a short route through Brundholme wood. There are outstanding views across to numerous fells, which look fantastic from the vantage point as you ascend on the edge of Latrigg fell. On reaching the summit there are far-reaching views, across Keswick, where you will see Derwent Water and Bassenthwaite Lake. There is water along the way for your dog. A good section of the walk is free from livestock, but there may be deer in the area. There is a short section of road.

How to get there – From Keswick follow the signs for Great Crosthwaite, the hospital and the Leisure pool. Crosthwaite car park is just before the hospital on the right hand side of Crosthwaite road.

Grid reference – NY 264240
Nearest post code – CA12 5PH

Parking – Pay and display at Crosthwaite or football club car park

Facilities – There are no facilities on this walk

You will need – Dog lead, dog bags

'he Walk

1 Leave the car park entrance and turn left. Turn left again almost nmediately onto the tarmac path. You will have the River Greta on your right .nd a cricket pitch on your left. Turn next left, on another tarmac path, with the ricket pitch still on your left on the edge of Fitz Park.

'urn left again and ascend passed a stone building. Pass a skate/BMX course n your left. Continue around a bend, where you will still have the skate track n your left, and a copse of trees on your right. At the end of the path, put your log on a lead and go through the gate. Turn right on the road. You will pass a :ul de sac on your right.

2 Shortly after, take the track on your left, which is signed Skiddaw. ascend on the track, which is part of the Cumbria Way. If you let your dog off ne lead, keep close control; listen for traffic, as it is an access road for one iouse. Also before reaching a bridge put your dog on the lead. It is fenced, but nere may be gaps, and the A66 dual carriage way is below. There is also a iouse beyond.

ihortly after crossing the bridge you will pass Spoony Green house. Your dog :an get a drink here, on the left from the stream. Go through the small gate, :nd continue to ascend on the track on the edge of a wood. The track will teepen as you continue. You will reach a gate on your right.

3 Go through the gate to enter Brundholme wood. Ascend on the path, which vill soon level out, cutting across the wooded hillside.

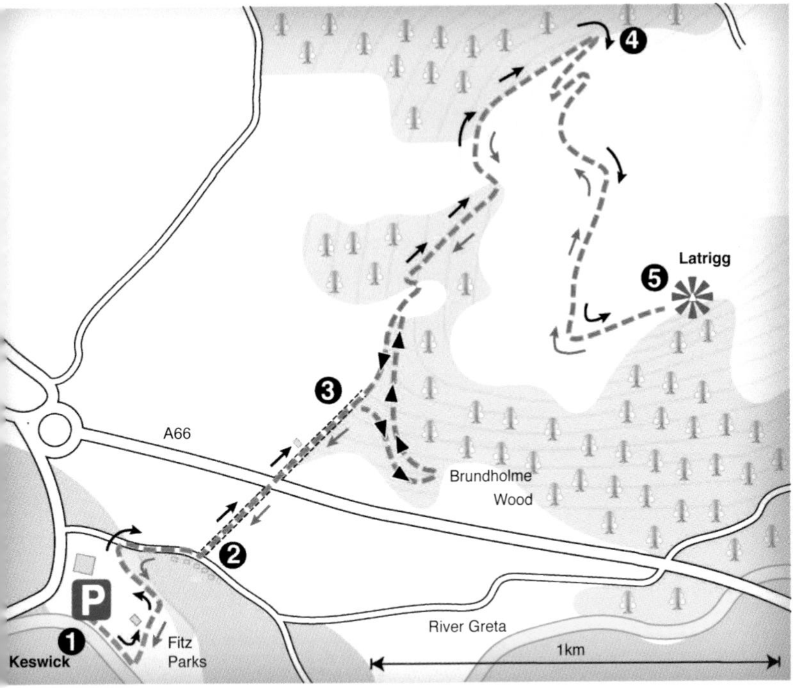

4
Latrigg
5
3
A66
Brundholme
Wood
2
P
1
Keswick
Fitz
Parks
River Greta
1km

Continue around a sharp left bend, ignoring the path on your right and ahead. On reaching the end of the path, pass through the gate and turn right. Continue to ascend. Where you turn around a left hand bend, your dog will fir water from a stream. Ignore a path, which forks to your right and continue straight ahead. After a while, and just before another left bend there is anothe spot for your dog to get a drink.

Just after the bend, you will reach a kissing gate. Put your dog on a lead, or under close control, as there may be livestock. Pass through the kissing gate, and continue straight ahead on a path, which cuts across the hillside. You wil gain amazing views on your left and behind, to several fells in the distance. Continue on the path, beside a stock fence on your left. Ignore a path through a gate on your left, and continue straight ahead.

❹ You will reach a finger post, signed for Latrigg summit. Take this path, which switches back on yourself, so you can continue to enjoy the views. Ascend again, on the path, which cuts across the hillside. The path has switchbacks to lessen the gradient. You will pass another path coming from your left.

Continue to ascend a little higher, still with the views on your right. You will reach a bench on your right where you can sit a while to soak up the atmosphere. Continue on the path, where you will turn a sharp left bend. This is the summit of Latrigg. When you are ready to turn back, remember to stay on the main path, ignoring paths on your left at the tight bend. Pass the benc and continue to descend. At the fork, ignore the path, which veers to your rig Continue to descend, retracing your steps.

You will reach the familiar kissing gate, where you enter back into the wood. As you continue, you will pass the path and gate on your left from your outbound route. Continue straight ahead, descending on the path. You will pass the gate on your left, where you entered into the wood. Continue straigh ahead, where you will leave the wood and cross over the bridge. Put your do on a lead, well in advance of reaching the road. For a guide, when you see th sheep pen on your right in the field. At the end of the track, turn right on the road. Pass the houses on your left, and just before you reach houses on you right, go through the familiar gate on your left. Continue on the tar mac path, passed the skate track, and then passed the cricket pitch. Turn right again on reaching another tar mac path, where you will soon reach the car park.

3. Friar's Crag

Medium - 4 miles - 2hr

This is a fabulous walk for you and your dog, starting with a splash for dogs in Derwent Water and going to the popular Friar's Crag, then back to the water's edge once more, before walking through beautiful woodlands. There is an uphill climb but it is well worth the effort as there as stunning views over Derwent Water and the many hills and mountains beyond. There are rivers and streams when away from Derwent Water so there is plenty of water along the way, for dogs to cool off and quench their thirst. There are sheep in parts of the walk and small sections of quiet road.

How to get there – From Keswick, follow the signs for Buttermere on the B5289. With Derwent Water on your right, you will pass a National Trust yard on your left, and a little further along the road the National Trust car park will be on your left hand side.

Grid reference - NY 272214

Parking – Pay and display, National Trust car park – Great Wood

Facilities – There is a dog-friendly café part way around

You will need – Dog leads, dog bags

he Walk

Put your dog on the lead to begin this walk. From the car park, head back ut onto the road at the entrance, crossing the road with care and descending ie steps into woodland. You will reach another path with a stream to your ght. Turn left here and cross the footbridge over a stream (not the ne to your right).

his path is parallel to the road on the left, ɔ take care if letting your dog off the lead. jnore the paths to the left and continue head until you reach the lake, turning right nto the path, which follows the water's dge.

ou can enjoy stunning views across the water the hills beyond, whilst your dog has a paddle the water. Continue on the path beside the 'oodland on your right and the water to your left. ıst after passing the woodland you will cross a ɔotbridge over a stream, and then walk beside the eld on the right and scrub to your left.

nce you enter into the pine trees, stay to the left. You will pass a lovely ench to your left. Once reaching a gate, keep dogs under close control or on

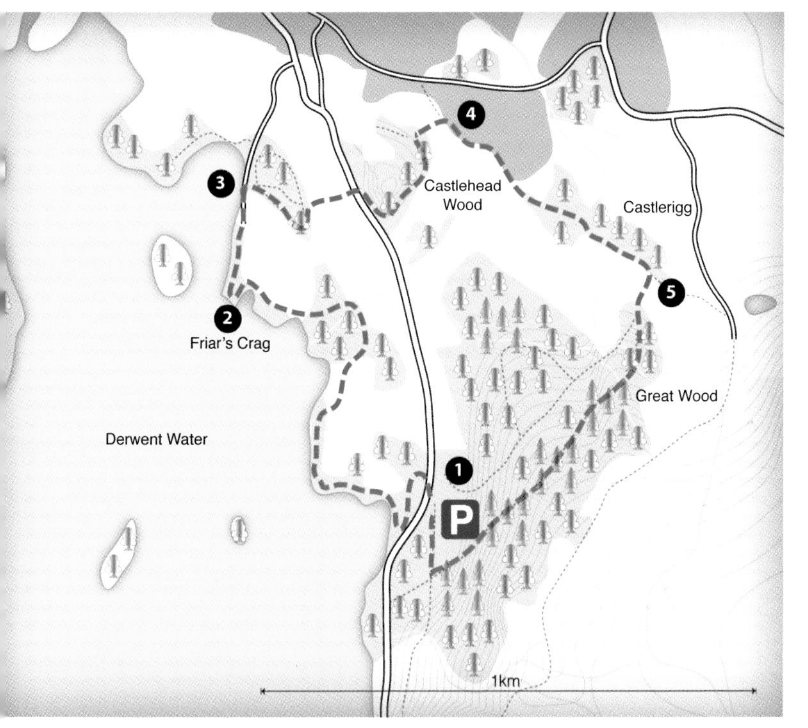

a lead as there may be sheep grazing in this sectio Follow the gravel path through the open fields, with views of Derwent Water to your left.

Stay to the path, passing a house on your left, and go through a gate to avoid the cattle grid. Follow on the access drive, keeping dogs under close control Pass between the hedgerows, taking a path to the left, and pass through the gate.

Keep to this path, passing through woodland carr, and a little further along cross a bridge over a stream. You will pass a lovely small meadow to the right, where on sunny days you can watch the butterflies.

As you reach another gate, ensure your dog is on a lead or under close control as there are sheep grazing for the next section of the walk. Pass through the gate and follow the path, crossing a couple of footbridges over streams, through farmla with parkland trees. You will soon be close to the water's edge, passing under some mature oak tree

Pass through another gate and then a few paces o take the path on the left with some steps, ascendin into the trees. Stay to the left and on reaching another path, turn left. On reaching a bench you will be at the point known a Friar's Crag. You will have wonderful views over Derwent Water and the hills beyond. ❷

Turn back on the path and go straight ahead, now with the water to your left Passing a couple of benches, staying to the wider track. Ignore the path to th right and continue, descending gradually. Keep dogs under close control as you reach an arched stone wall feature, with a plaque on your right, as there is an access road ahead. Continue following the split rail fence on your right

When you reach the road, stay to the gravel path and continue ahead, passi a stone building on your left. You will now be beside Derwent Water once more. ❸ Continue ahead towards the harbour, passing steps on the right. Take the second-to-last set of steps before the building ahead, which leads to the access road. Once on the road, you will see a footpath on the opposit side to your right. Take this footpath with woodland to your left and farmland your right. You will reach another path, turning right into the woodland. You w have farmland to your right through the trees.

Continue along this path, passing a narrow path to your right, and once at th end turn left. After a short distance you will reach a junction of paths. Take th path on the right, passing between farmland, with a hedgerow to your left an stock fencing to your right. Put your dog on a lead, before nearing the end o the path, as there is a busy road ahead.

At the end of the path, ascend the steps and cross the road, with care. Pass through a gap in the stone wall on the opposite side into woodland and turn right. Keep your dog on a lead at first as the path parallels the road.

Once you see a path to the left, follow this ascending into the woodland, leaving the road behind. Follow the well-worn path through the trees. Ignore a path to the right and continue straight ahead. The path will descend and just as it levels out once more you will pass a rocky crag to your left.

Keep to the path straight ahead, ignoring a path that veers to the left. The path will descend a little more steeply and you will reach a kissing gate in the corner. Pass through the kissing gate, following the path between farmland on the tar-mac path. Put your dog on a lead before reaching the end of the path, and turn right onto the quiet road. ❹ Follow this road, which ascends, passing houses to your left. On reaching the end, you will pass Springs Farm on your right and then a dog-friendly café to your left.

Continue straight ahead, passing through a gate into woodland, ascending or a stone path with a river to your left. When you reach the brow of the hill turn right, walking between the stone walls. ❺ The path will ascend once more, quite steeply to begin with. You will have the edge of the woodland on your right and farmland on your left, with stunning views of Derwent Water where gaps in the hedge allow.

You will pass a mast to your right. A little further along, just before reaching a stone wall, turn right. This path descends now, with fantastic views on your right across farmland, woodlands and Derwent Water to the many hills beyond. On entering into the forest, the path will descend quite steeply, crossing a small stream. Continue on the path, ignoring a path to the right. Yo will reach another path, where you turn left, ascending at first.

The path will level out and it cuts across the hillside, passing through beautif mixed woodland. You will start to descend, but only gradually at first. There are a few streams, which pass across the path. The path will become a little rough and stony, and will start to descend a little more steeply. There are many ferns on the woodland floor in places. Once reaching the end of the path, turn right passing a vehicle barrier, and continue straight ahead ignorin a path to the left. Put your dogs on the leads here, as the car park is just a little further ahead.

0 to carry 5

4. Newlands Beck

Easy - 4.5 miles - 2h

This is a lovely walk which passes through quiet lanes, beautiful woodlands with moss covered rocky boulders, and scenic farmland with mature trees. There are stunning mountain views as you walk in the valley amongst the hills, beside a beautiful river with gorse bushes and trees on both sides. There are sheep in parts of this walk and some quiet roads. There are lots o opportunities for dogs to get water along the way.

How to get there – From Keswick take the A66 to Portinscale, pass through the village and follow signs for Grange. At a junction turn right signed for Skelgill. The car park is on the left hand side.

Grid reference – NY 245211
Nearest post code – CA12 5UE

Parking – Free in the parking bay. Get there early, as there are limited spaces.

Facilities – There is a café along the way and dogs are welcome on the patio.

You will need – Dog leads, dog bags

The Walk

1 From the car park face the road and turn right, passing Guther Scale on he left and hills to the right. There are mountain views across the valley to the eft. On meeting another road on a bend turn left to descend the hill, passing ovely mature oaks on the left.

Go through a gate at the side of the cattle grid. Just afterwards, as the oad bends sharply, take the footpath signed Hawes End. Passing a yew and mature beech, follow on the path between the trees. There is some exposed rock on the path and outcrops on the right. Follow the stone wall on the left. When you each a road take the kissing gate on he opposite side, signed Portinscale, and follow between the fences passing through mixed coniferous and broadleaved woodland.

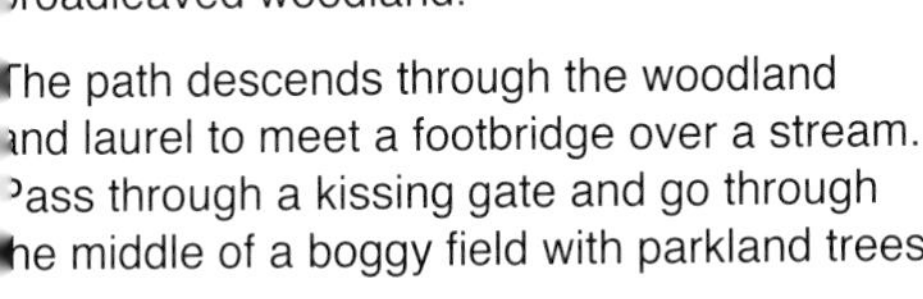

The path descends through the woodland and laurel to meet a footbridge over a stream. Pass through a kissing gate and go through he middle of a boggy field with parkland trees.

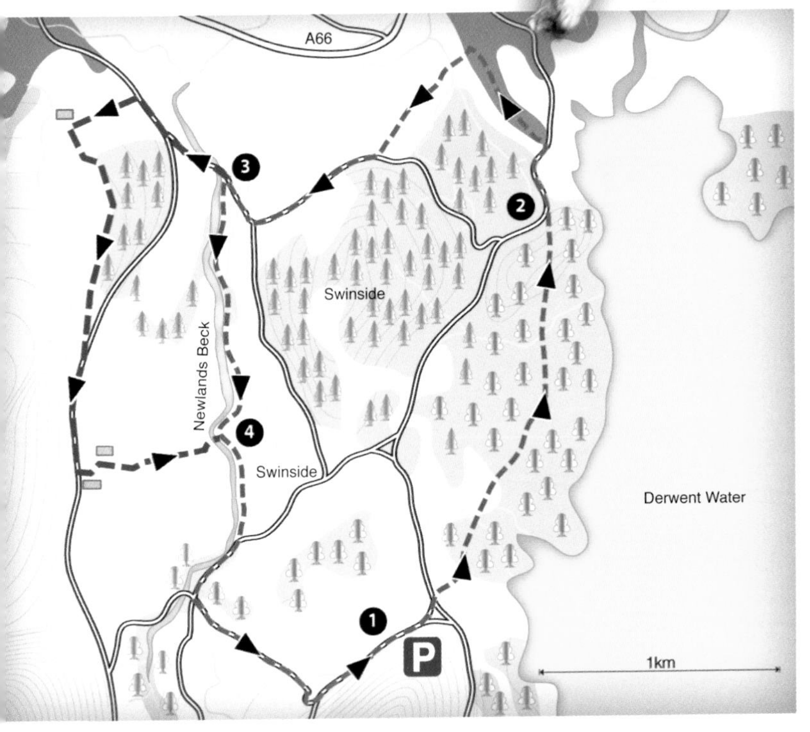

Passing through another kissing gate, continue on the stone path through woodland. Pass through another gate next to the driveway of Lingholm and continue straight on, taking the footpath signed for Keswick beside a lovely stone wall on the right. Just before the end of the stone wall take the footpath on the left, on a gravel path through the mixed woodland and rhododendron.

The path will begin to incline a little. Further on, ensure your dog is on the lea as when the path declines again you will reach a road.

Turn right on the road passing a marina and a footpath on the right. Continue on the pavement, passing Dandelion Café where dogs are welcome in the outside seating area. As you pass another entrance to the Dandelion Café tak the footpath on the opposite side of the road, walking along an access road fc houses. The path will open out after passing several houses, where you will have terrific views. Ignore a footpath on the left and continue for some time. Look out for another footpath on the left, which passes down the side of gardens. Cross a bridge over a ditch and then pass through a gate and follow the obvious path through the middle of a field with mountain views in all directions.

Pass a farm gate on the right and then take the gate immediately after walkin between a fence and a beech hedge. Pass a house on the right and ascend the steps, pass through a gate and turn right, passing Yew Tree cottage, a farmhouse, and buildings on your right. You will be walking along a sealed road with fields on both sides and lovely views of the surrounding mountains. When you reach another road turn right. Just before going over a lovely stone road bridge take the gate on the left, signed for Stair.

*If this footpath is not available because of flooding/erosion follow the directions on page 20 - 3a.

Continue along the river embankment of Newlands Beck, passing through the valley with views of Catbells on the left and farmland to both sides. There are lovely panoramic views of the hills and mountains here as you continue along the river bank. There are trees on both sides of the river and some gorse.

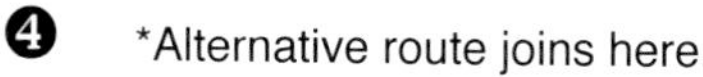

*Alternative route joins here.

Pass a stone bridge on the right and continue following the river. When you reach a farm gate and a small gate, pass through the small gate, continuing with the river. You will pass through another gate ahead and then a little furthe on you will reach a road.

Putting your dogs on leads, pass through the gate onto the road, turning right. At the end of the football field on your right take the quiet road on the lef signed for Skelgill Farm, passing between farm fields. A little further along the road you will pass between houses and farm buildings. Staying on the road, g through the farm gate and continue straight ahead, with views to your left of Swinside and Bassenthwaite Lake. You will soon reach the lay-by where you have parked your car.

A - Continue over Little Braithwaite Bridge. Ascend on the road. You will pass farm building on your right, and then houses left and right. Continue on the ad. You will have views on your right, across the valley to the fells beyond. n reaching another road, turn right. After about 200 yards look out for a otpath on your left. Keep your dog on a lead, or under close control. Ascend e steps and go through the gate. Continue to ascend beside a stock fence on our right. You will see Bassenthwaite Lake in the distance on your right.

fter a short distance you will merge with another path. Continue straight head towards a farmhouse. Pass a stone shelter and continue beside a stone all. Very soon after, pass through a farm gate. Continue straight ahead etween a stone wall and stock fence. Pass the farm house beyond the wall, nd go through a farm gate. Pass beside a farm building on your right, and en go through a farm gate on your left. Continue to ascend gently on a stone ath. On reaching the corner of the field, pass through the gate and turn left.

ou will gain wonderful views on your left and behind as you continue to scend. Stay to your left, where you will continue on the path, which cuts cross the hillside of Barrow fell. You will follow a block of woodland, which is ver on your left. Ignore the path, which ascends the fell, and veers slightly ght. As you continue, the wood will become further away for a while. On eaching close beside the wood, it is predominantly Scot's pine. You will begin descend. When you pass the wood, put your dog on a lead, as there is a oad ahead. On reaching the road, turn right. Stay on the right hand side of the oad, to face oncoming cars. Shortly after, take the track on your left, which is gned Uzzicar Farm.

escend on the track. Continue around a left bend on the track, and head for e farm house. Pass farm buildings on your right, and turn left before reaching e farm house gate. Stay on the track, passing Low Uzzicar house on your ft. Continue to descend gently, between stock fences, and remnants of an d hedgerow. There are wonderful views left and right.
ou will weave your way between fields. At the end of the track, go through the ate and cross the bridge. Turn right.

Both routes merge here. Now follow from number 4 back on page 19 to read irections back to the car park.

5. Castle Crag

Medium - 3.8 miles - 2hrs 30m

This walk follows part of the Cumbrian Way along the beautiful Borrowdale Valley, walking beside the river Derwent and amongst some stunning oak woodland, passing around Castle Crag. As you climb a little higher you will have some wonderful panoramic views as you pass the foot of Low and High Scawdel. There are streams and rivers throughout the walk to keep your dog energised. There are sheep in many parts of the walk, but this one really is worth the effort it takes to keep your dog under close control.

How to get there – From Keswick turn onto the B5289 (Honister Pass) signed for Buttermere. On reaching the village of Rosthwaite turn right following the signs for parking. You can park just before the Yew Tree Farm tea room.

Grid reference – NY 257148
Nearest post code - CA12 5XB

Parking – Pay and display car park, Village hall or National Trust

Facilities – There are toilets beside the car park and a tea room at Yew Tree Farm.

You will need – Dog leads, dog bags

The Walk

1 From the car park go onto the road and turn right, passing between buildings with a tea room on the right. Cross the farmyard, then follow between stone walls in the valley, surrounded by stunning scenery.

On reaching the river take the path right to follow with the river on your left. Cross over a lovely stone bridge and turn right. When you reach two gates go through the gate on the right staying with the river. Keep your dog under close control or on a lead as you will be amongst sheep.

Walk amongst the stunning scenery surrounded by hills and mountains in this lovely valley, passing under mature ash and alder trees. The path soon leaves the river, veering to the left and passing a ditch as it flows beneath the path. Walking under mature oak trees you will pass a stile on your left a little further along, go through a kissing gate and continue with a stock fence to your right and an old stone wall on your left. Walk through the mixed deciduous woodland, on a gently sloping path, passing several streams.

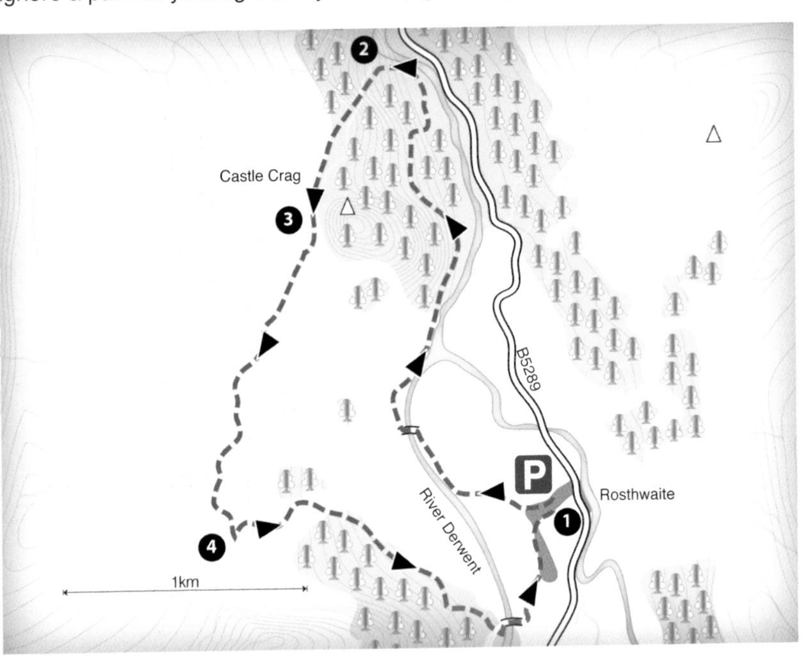

Follow up and over the exposed bedrock amongst the trees, with rocky boulders strewn across the woodland floor green with mosses. There are rough grassland meadows and the path begins to incline. You will pass a small quarry on the left then through a gap in the stone wall. Continue straight ahead, ignoring a narrow path on your left and then a little further along, ignore a path on your right and just after, ignore a path on your left. Continue to ascend and then turn right when you meet with another path, following the way marker signed for Grange. Descending a little now, pass through a gap in the stone wall and turn right. The path will meet with the river once more. As you leave the river the path will incline. Pass through a gate and descend toward a bridge. ❷ Turn left before the bridge on the stone path ascending once again. You will now see coniferous trees to your left and woodland to your right. Cross a footbridge and turn left with coniferous trees now on your right. The path is now a well made rocky path, which ascends a little more steeply. Pass through a gate where the landscape opens out into stunning hillside scenery to your right and a stone wall to your left. There are some scattered trees with rare juniper to your right growing out of the rock face.

Continue on your ascent ignoring a path to the left, a little further along, and continue straight ahead into the saddle of the hillside. ❸ Have a rest at the summit on reaching a gate into a sheep fold, to the left of the path. Here the views are truly stunning in every direction. This is a great place to stop for a picnic. Continue over the other side passing the sheep fold on your left. Just after the sheepfold ignore a desire line on the left and then ignore a footpath on the left, which both lead to a gate in the stone wall and then immediately after take the path on the left, which leads through the valley ahead, leaving the wider, stone track. Cross a bridge over a river and turn left passing through a gate. Stay on this obvious worn path and do not turn left. A little further along, pass through a gate and cross a bridge over another river. Stay with the stone wall to your left until you reach a small gate. ❹ Pass through the gate and follow the stone wall on the left.

Descend the hill part way down, then, as you pass the trees on the right, veer right for 100 yards until you see a worn path. Turn on this path to continue towards a stone wall ahead and to your right. The path will get a little boggy here. Go through a gate and over a footbridge crossing a stream. Now follow the stone wall on your right. Ignore a ladder stile and follow the obvious worn path descending with a stream below and lovely woodland to your left. Pass a ruined sheepfold/shelter on the left and continue; you will pass through a gate. Continue through woods between stock fences with farmland on the left in the valley. Ascend again to pass over a small crag, then go down again ignoring a gate on the right and continue to follow the path. Another descent will bring you into the bottom of the valley.

Pass a farmyard on the left and go through a kissing gate, putting dogs on leads. At the end of the stone wall on you left, turn left onto a quiet road and left again. Cross over the road bridge and pass houses in the village. Turn left where the road bends to the right. Pass through a gate and then pass a row of cottages and go through a farm gate staying to the right of the field. Pass through another gate in the corner of the field and continue diagonally left. Pass through another kissing gate, staying to the right of the field with lovely views still of the craggy hill tops. Pass through another gate, turning right onto a track, and then left on the quiet road. Pass cottages and farm buildings then you will reach the tea room once more on your left. Follow the bend, to the right of the road back to your car.

6. Derwent Water

Medium - 7.2 miles - 3hr

This walk is superb. It passes through woodland pasture, woodland, forest and meadows, through the beautiful Grange village crossing farmland and then beside Derwent water with wonderful mountain views. There are plenty of streams along the way to quench his thirst. There are short sections of road and there are sheep grazing. From this car park you can also visit the Bowder stone, an enormous glacial boulder, following the signs as you enter the car park for a short walk through delightful woodland.

How to get there – Take the B5289 from Keswick signed for Buttermere. On leaving the edge of Derwent Water and passing the road bridge on the right for Grange village, look out for the National Trust car park on the left hand side of the road.

Grid reference - NY 253168
Nearest postcode – CA12 5

Parking – Pay and display, National Trust car park

Facilities – Toilets and cafes in Grange Village

You will need – Dog leads, dog bags

he Walk

From the furthest parking bay from the ·ad, face the direction of the road and turn ʒht, passing through the kissing gate. There ·e two of them so take the one on the left, hich has the stone weight. There may be ıeep here so keep your dog under close ɔntrol. Continue on the worn path through the ees, which will clear into woodland pasture. You ill head towards a large boulder. Cross a stream nd follow the worn path that ascends with a glade to ɔur right.

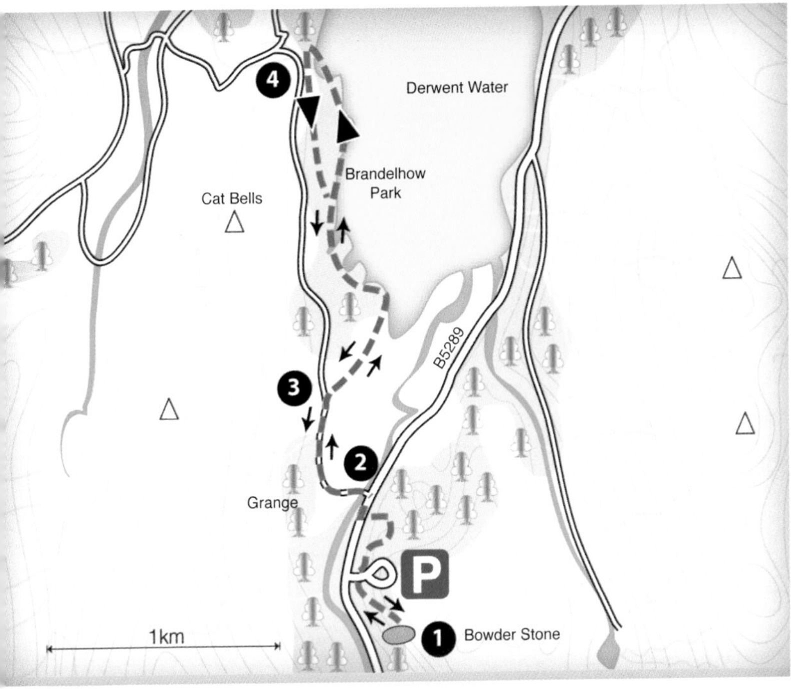

ass the exposed rock on your left and as you enter ·e open grassland you will pass an old quarried area ith a small cave on your right. Continue on the path straight ahead, ignoring ıe path to the left. Head for the round boulder-like hills ahead, passing etween the bracken with scattered trees and gorse. You will ascend slightly nd just before the path levels out you will meet with another worn path. Turn ·ft here and descend once more. There is plenty of water along the way ere for dogs, as there are many streams that flow into a boggy area. Take path on the right just before the hawthorn, passing between gorse and a ɔcky outcrop. The path will descend again, following the sharp bend to the ght, and then descends a little more steadily passing between the exposed

rock. Put your dog on a lead, as there is a busy road ahead. Pass through a kissing gate, crossing immediately and with care onto the other side of the road, and turn right walking along the narrow footpath.

❷ When you reach the stone road bridge on the left, cross it, taking care as there is no footpath. Once over the bridge turn left into Grange village: you will pass toilets on the left and there are a couple of cafes along the way. Continue on this road, passing through the village. There are lovely views of mountains on both sides of the village. Continue on this road, ignoring a footpath to the left just before Borrowdale Gates Hotel. Pass the hotel on your right and Tor House on your left. You will reach woodland on both sides of the road. On passing a farmyard on your right, take the next footpath on the right. ❸ You must keep your dog under close control through the farmland. The path follows a river on the right where dogs can get water. The river bends away from the path, where you will now be walking through the middle of the field. Cross over a footbridge and follow the stoned path.

Go through a kissing gate and continue straight ahead through farmland with scots pine trees. Pass through a farm gate, cross a stream, and continue straight ahead, passing through gorse and onto a boardwalk over a boggy area. Continue through the silver birch and hawthorn trees. Once reaching another path, turn left where you will come close to Derwent Water. Cross another couple of boardwalks along this path to avoid the boggy sections, passing amongst the trees and scrub with rocky crags.

Cross another boardwalk. You will then go through a gate into woodlands following the gravel path near to the lakeside. Pass over a series of small footbridges over streams. The path will weave in and out of sight of Derwent Water. When you reach a house turn right on the quiet access track, keeping dogs under close control, heading towards another house. Pass through a kissing gate and follow the path with the house to the left and a shed to the right. You will meet with the lake once more, passing gorse to your left. Cross a footbridge over a stream.

Head for the gate along the water's edge, beside the shale bank. You will reach a copse of scots pines; turn left, passing under the pines. You will meet two paths ahead. Take the lower path, passing a jetty and a couple of picnic benches. Continue along this path beside the lake. Here there is beautiful mixed woodland, rocky crags covered in moss, and many streams entering the lake. Cross a series of small footbridges where you will see pebble beaches. You can sit a while and rest, enjoying the water.

You will pass a wooden carving of a pair of hands on your right. A little further on pass through a gate beside another jetty, and turn immediately left, beside the stone wall. Pass through another gate, and follow the path straight ahead with a wet boggy field on your left. Pass through another gate further along and continue on the path, passing an adventure centre to the left.

Ascend a hill and once through a gate turn left onto a sealed path. Pass between two walls and through a gate, avoiding the cattle grid, and continue towards the house. ❹ Take the path to the right of the house, and then pass through another two gates. You will walk amongst mature beech, cutting along the hillside with views to the left of Derwent Water and the mountains that surround it. On passing the beech trees you will reach more widely spaced mixed woods with gorse. Cross a stream and pass a stone building on your left. Cross another stream and continue on another ascent, ignoring a stile on your right. Pass through a gate into woodland with some coniferous trees. Although you have now left the agricultural areas there still may be sheep grazing here. Cross a stream and once reaching a fork, take the left path, which descends a little further along. Ignore the paths to the left and right and continue straight ahead. There are lots of small streams to cross where your dog will have plenty of opportunities to drink.

You will eventually see the lake again to your left. Once you reach near to the lake, on meeting another path turn right heading away from the water and go up the steps to your left, before reaching the gate ahead. Follow the well-worn path through the trees, passing through a gate and turning left which leads back to a familiar path to retrace your steps. Cross the bridge and pass a house, going back through the gate. Remember to turn left once you reach the second house, meeting with the water's edge once more. Follow this path passing again over the boardwalks, and on reaching close to the end of the lake once more turn right on the grassy path (if you reach another gate beside the water, you have missed your turning). Follow this path back, passing through a farm gate and then further on a kissing gate onto the road.

On reaching the road, turn left and descend to the village once more, crossing the road bridge and turning right. Once you pass the house on the left cross the busy road and pass through the gate. Ascend between the exposed rocks and continue on this path, which bends to the left. Once near the top, just before the path levels, take the path on the right and begin to descend. Crossing a wet area again, continue straight ahead passing the exposed rock outcrop, where you will see the car park ahead.

7. Thirlmere

Medium - 3 miles - 1hr 30mir

This is a lovely linear walk with a small detour to change the walk a little on your return. You will walk close to the water's edge for a time and pass through some fantastic mature woodlands and forest. There is a steep incline that brings you to the top of Great How, giving stunning panoramic views of mountain peaks and over Thirlmere. There are sheep in some areas of this walk but there are no roads. Your dog will find water at several places along the way

How to get there – Follow the A591 from Grasmere to Keswick and look for the lay-by on the left hand side of the road, just after passing the Swirls car park on the right.

Grid Reference – NY 315169

Parking – Pay and display in the lay-by

Facilities – There are no facilities

You will need – Leads, dog bags.

ıe Walk

From the parking bay follow the steps down ıd take the gate on the left. There may be eep grazing here, so ensure you have your dog ı a lead or under close control. Follow the stone ıth across the field, which meets with a stock ɿnce and river on your left. The path descends wards the reservoir, passing through a gate.

ɔu will now be passing through predominantly silver ·ch woodland with some beech. Continue on the main ıth, with some gradual slopes following parallel to the ‹e. Your dogs will soon find water as you walk close Thirlmere and from streams that pass under the path. ɜfore the path ascends with a sharp right turn, take a ırrow path on the left indicated by a way marker with a ɹe arrow, passing beneath the mature oaks and pines.

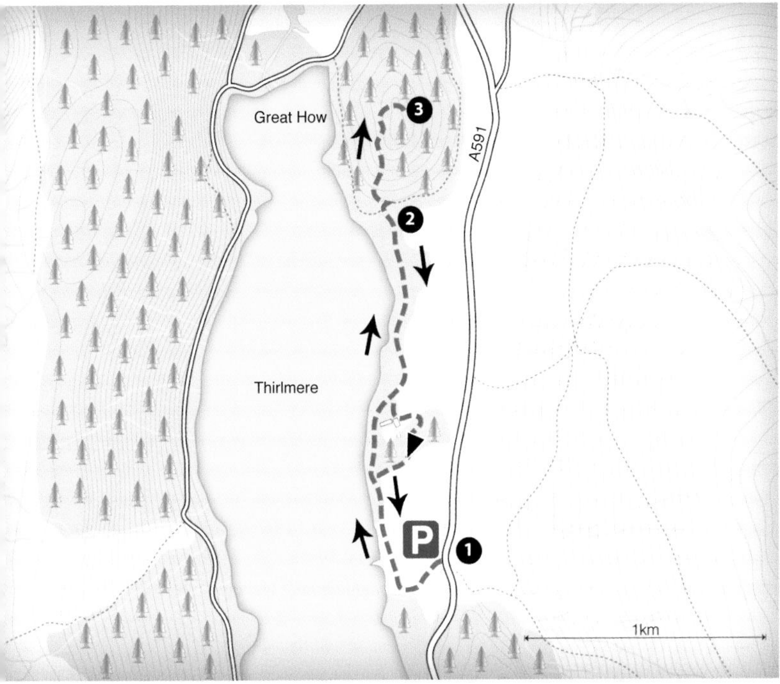

ɔllow this narrow path, passing through a kissing gate :o woodland with mature oaks and beech. Cross over the roots of a large ɜe then pass over a footbridge to cross a stream. A boulder path gets you :ross a boggy section. Then continue on the obvious worn path, passing a ·ge house to your far right. Pass over another couple of footbridges and past e stump of a very large tree on your left that has been felled. The woodlands

open up a little here, where there are grassy glades in places and a pebble beach where you can sit and enjoy the water. The path veers away from the lake. Then turn left onto a wider track, where you will now be entering an old pinetum - a collection of conifer trees such as cedar, redwood and monkey puzzle. Continue on the path through a gate and start to incline on the wider stoned path. There may be sheep grazing here.

Begin to descend again. You will pass through a small plantation of Scots pines. As the path inclines once more you will be met by beautiful views of the mountain peaks ahead and right. The path will bend sharply right, and then further ahead, after another steady incline and immediately after anothe sharp bend to the right, you will see a grassy path on the left that ascends th hillside. ❷ Take this path to begin your climb, which will rise high above the lake, passing through mature oak woods with glacial boulders.

The path will get rocky as you climb higher, following the way marker and a sign for Great How summit. Once you reach a level grassy path turn right. You may need to ensure that your dog is under close control as there are roc faces with drops on the other side as you approach a bench.

❸ The views here are stunning and you can rest for a while and take it all ir The highest point can be reached just a little further on by taking a left turn, from your sitting position on the bench, on the slightly worn track. You will se a mound of rocks that people have placed. Here you will see panoramic view that are worth all the effort it has taken to get here. Now it is mostly back dov the way that you came, with a little detour for a change in scenery. Once you have descended the steeper section and reached the main track, remember turn right.

Follow this path and pass back through the gate into the pinetum. Follow the path now, ignoring the path to the left. Pass through a gate and, ensuring yo dog is on a lead, stay on this path, passing houses on your right. Pass throu the gate and onto a quiet road. Take the path on the opposite side, ignoring the path that leads to Dale Head Hall.

Following the path between the trees, pass through a gate following the old stone wall on your right. Then pass through another gate, keeping with the stone wall. There may be sheep grazing here. Pass through another gate where you will soon meet with a familiar path. Keep to this path now, passing two lovely waterfalls on your right, and soon you will reach back to your car.

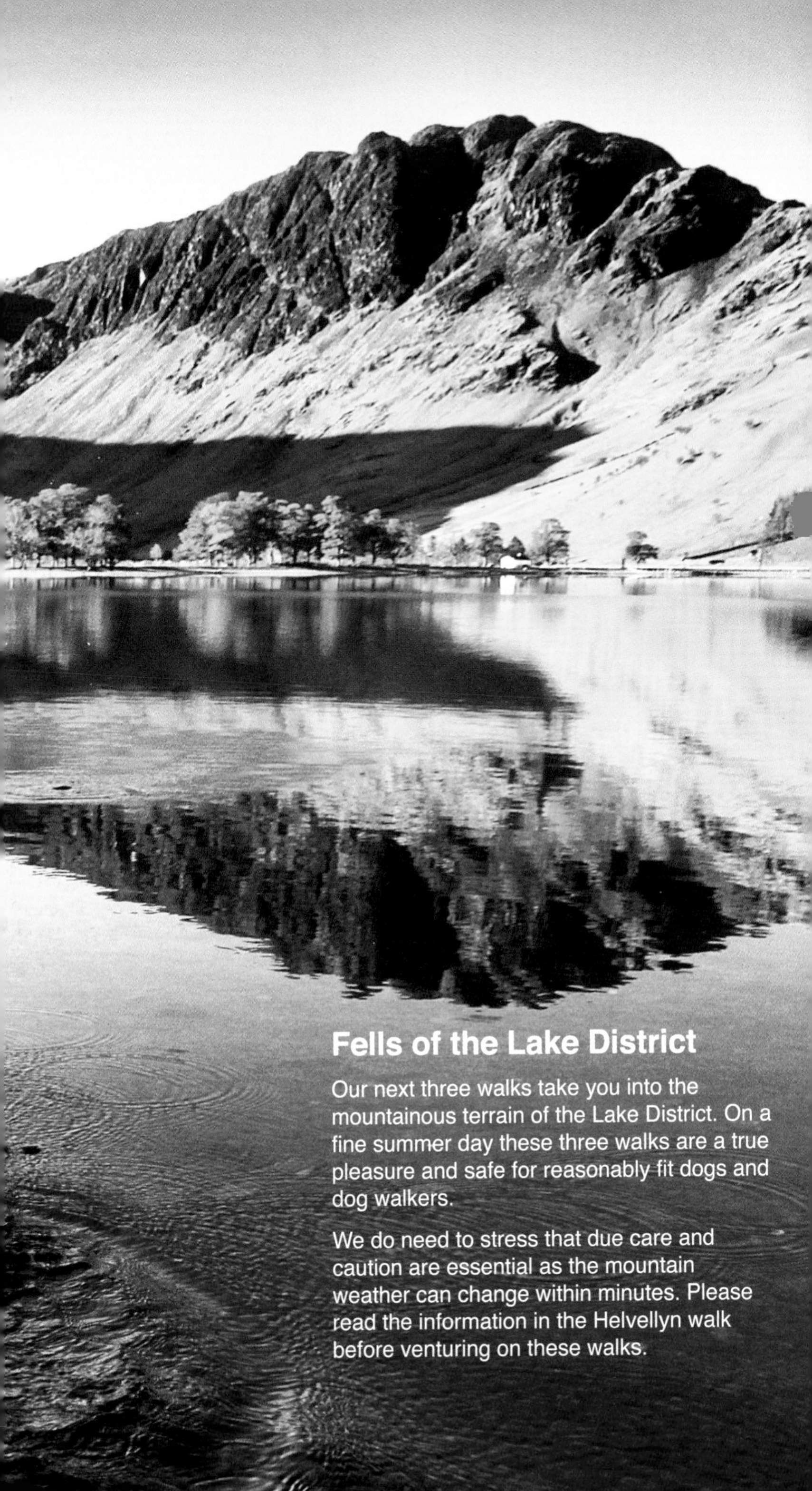

Fells of the Lake District

Our next three walks take you into the mountainous terrain of the Lake District. On a fine summer day these three walks are a true pleasure and safe for reasonably fit dogs and dog walkers.

We do need to stress that due care and caution are essential as the mountain weather can change within minutes. Please read the information in the Helvellyn walk before venturing on these walks.

8. Helvellyn

Challenging - 6.2 miles - 5h

This a brilliant fell walk, for fit and healthy dogs. You will need a clear day, as the effort of the climb deserves the glorious views from the top. There are sheep throughout most of the walk with gravel paths on the descent, so if yo need to have your dog on the lead amongst sheep it can get a little tricky on the way down. There are no scrambles, and the paths are clearly defined. The woods on the way back are fantastic, with many streams and rivers. Avoid a hot day as there is no shelter until you reach the woods on the last section.

How to get there - Follow the A591 from Grasmere to Keswick and look for Swirls car park on the right hand side of the road.

Grid Reference – NY 316168

Parking – Pay and display in Swirls car park

Facilities – There are toilets in the car park

You will need – Dog leads, water for your dog

MOUNTAIN SAFETY

Weather can be a serious concern. You need a clear day with good conditions, and unless you have mountain walking experience it is better to choose summer months with longer daylight hours

This is a big day out, and you and your dog will need to be fit and healthy

Leave plenty of time to do the walk, at least six hours of daylight time

Your dog will need to be kept under close control when not on a lead

You will need to wear sturdy footwear and take plenty of food and water.

Keep to the surfaced paths at all times

Check the specific mountain weather forecast at:
www.metoffice.gov.uk
(choose the Lake District area for specific details of conditions)

Again, unless you have mountain walking experience (which includes map and compass) it is better to wait for that near perfect day to take on these wonderful challenges

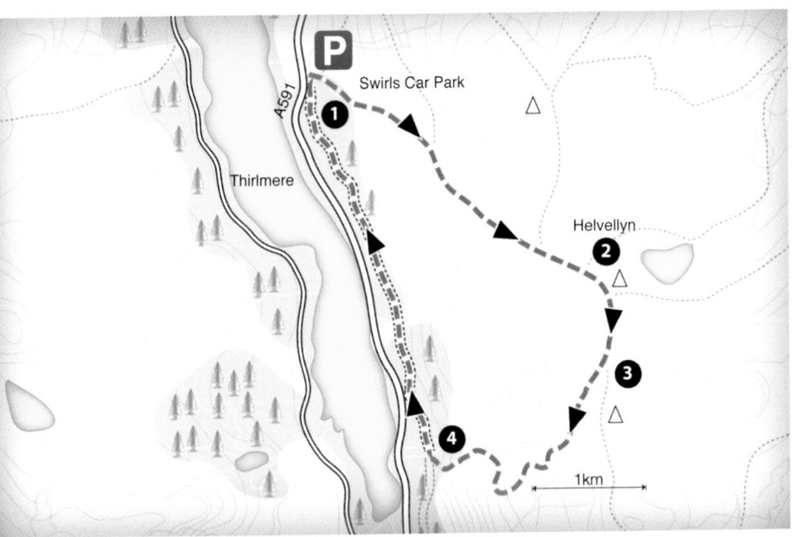

The Walk

❶ From the car park, head to the furthest end from the road and take the footpath. Cross the bridge over the stream, then go through the kissing gate. Stay on the stone path alongside the stream. Ignore a grassy path to your right and continue straight ahead.

Pass through a gate where your ascent begins, crossing a couple of narrow footbridges over streams. The path will get quite rough and rocky, and you will follow a stone wall on your right for a while.

Pass over another stream and cross a footbridge over a river. Then pass through a gate where the path veers left and leaves the stone wall behind, rising up the hillside passing scattered trees. Stay on this path, which has a series of cobble steps and switch-backs to lessen the gradient.

As you climb, you will have stunning views across Thirlmere and to the fells beyond. As you approach a rocky outcrop the path will become quite steep, with steps for most of the way. Once over this you will have done the hard work - the gradient of the path will lessen and become gravel.

Where the path levels out, you will see the summit. There is another, gentle climb, staying on the main path. When you see a trig point ahead call your dog close as there is a very steep edge here. ❷ When you reach the trig point at another path, turn right. There are stunning views in all directions here on a clear day, surrounded by fells with Ullswater on your left.

When you reach a stone wall cross shelter giving protection from the wind, you can take a well-deserved rest . Once rested, get back on the path with the shelter to your left. ❸ Take the path to the right of the fell top, which will be stone/gravel for most of the descent. You will see three paths ahead of you

in the distance. You will be following the path to the right as you descend.

You will gain fabulous views of Thirlmere once more on your right as you descend. The path will again have a series of switch-backs and some steps to lessen the gradient. After going over a small section of exposed rock the path bends to the right, and you will soon see forest ahead in the distance. This is where you are headed and you will see the path as it zig-zags down the hillside.

The path will become stone cobbles, and will reach near to a river on your right which flows down the face of the fell. Here your dog can cool off and get a well-deserved drink. The path will meet with the forest on your right. Follow the fence line continuing on your descent. You will pass through a large gate, into the forest. Stay on the cobble path, still descending.

❹ When you meet with another path, turn right, taking the level path signed for Swirls. Pass through the gate and follow the forest track. You will pass several streams and rivers that flow off the many rock faces to your right and under the path. Your dog will enjoy cooling off on hot days here in the pools.

The path has gentle slopes and you will see Thirlmere through gaps in the trees to your left. There are many shades of green here: the forest floor has varied flowers depending on the season, mosses, ferns and lichens. Ignore a path to the left and ahead which descends, and continue straight ahead, where the path narrows and inclines through a kissing gate and over a bridge to cross a stream. There is a forest clearing where you will have stunning views of Thirlmere. Cross another bridge over a stream, where you will see a waterfall on your right.

You will pass through another kissing gate to enter beautiful woodlands with rocky boulders and several streams crossing the path. There are many ferns, mosses and woodland flowers. You will pass stunning rock faces and there are gradual slopes. Cross another footbridge over a river and go past the rocky outcrops, following the blue way-markers.

When you reach the main forest track again, turn right. You will again pass a series of streams flowing down the rock faces to your right, with pools below for your dog to cool off in. A little further on you will pass through a gate beside a ladder stile. Stay on this main path, where you will reach close to the main road. Call your dog close or on a lead as you will be soon approaching the car park. Pass through the gate at the stone wall and then through another gate to the car park.

9. Cat Bells

Challenging - 3.5 miles - 2hr

This walk is a must for those who like a challenge, climbing high for absolutel fantastic views of Derwent Water and the surrounding fells. There are a couple of scrambles to do, which are easy but not recommended for old arthritic dogs. There are sheep throughout this walk so if you have a dog that needs to stay on the lead, take care when doing the scramble sections on the way up.

How to get there – From Keswick take the A66 to Portinscale passing through the village and follow signs for Grange. At a junction turn right signed for Skelgill. The car park is on the left hand side.

Grid reference – NY 245211
Nearest post code – CA12 5UE

Parking – Free in the parking bay. Get there early, as there are limited spaces

Facilities – There are no facilities on this walk

You will need – Dog leads, dog bags and water for your dog

The Walk

1 Facing the road, turn right to take the footpath which ascends immediately, cutting along the hillside between bracken and giving views ahead right from the start. As you climb a little more you will be in view of Derwent Water on the other side.

Keep ascending, veering to the right when the path ahead begins to descend. The views are truly amazing as you see more of Derwent Water and the surrounding fells and mountains.

The path has a couple of switch backs, and then if you look behind you and to the left you will have views of Bassenthwaite Lake. There is a bit of a scramble up and over a rocky section to bring you up onto the ridge.

2 Once on the ridge you will have fantastic panoramic views of sculpted fells and mountains in all directions, keeping Derwent Water in your sights to the left. You are now on top of Skelgill Bank. Continue along this ridge, where you will see a well worn path going down to the left ahead. The steep hill straight on is Cat Bells. If it looks too daunting for you or your dog or the weather has turned, the path on the left is your escape route.

Once reaching the path on the left you can choose option A) to continue your climb to Cat Bells or option B) to turn left to start your descent.

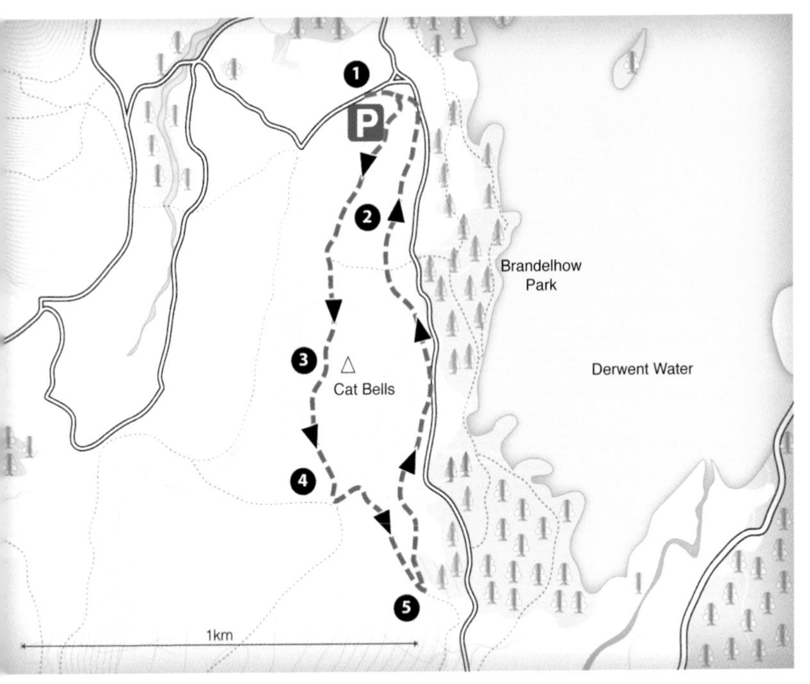

A. Continue heading towards the steeper hill on the path, which snakes around the rugged rocks. There is another small section to scramble. Walk over the rocky sections, choosing the route that you are comfortable with.

❸ Once at the summit you can rest and enjoy the terrific views, surrounded by fells and looking over Derwent Water. Once rested, take the path to the left and continue on. It is a gradual descent to begin with.

To your left you will see the end of Derwent Water, and new views ahead. Continue on this path where after a while the path veers to the left. Keep to this path and not the one that begins to ascend once more. ❹ The path is gravel with some staggered steps, and then, on the steeper sections, stone slab. You will reach a left turn with stone slab steps. Take this turning, now with Derwent Water ahead and to your right and with forest to your near right. ❺

On reaching the forest keep going straight ahead, ignoring the path on the right. You will be ascending slightly now, where you will soon reach a memorial stone bench at a rocky crag. A little further along your dogs can enjoy a stream as it trickles down the hillside. The path will now descend gently, passing another welcome stream for dogs, as you reach a gorse patch. You will meet with the road, staying with the path, passing a rock face on the left and back up a steep ascent to begin with. The path will level out and you will soon see a path to the left where option B meets your path.

B. Follow the path on the left, descending the hill a little steeply in places until you reach a wider stoned path. Turn left on this path.

Both options are combined at this point.

You will now be walking parallel to a road a little further down on the right, with Derwent Water beyond this. Pass through a section of gorse and a rocky crag to the left, walking amongst the bracken and grassland cutting along the hillside. You will see a steep path to the left as you near buildings below to your right. Take this path, where you will soon see around a bend that this is the path from which you began. Continue descending, passing a path on the right until you reach the parking bay.

10. Low Fell

Challenging - 4 miles - 2hrs

This is a beautiful linear walk with amazing views across Crummock Water and Loweswater and the surrounding fells after a moderate ascent. You will pass some lovely mature trees along the way and a couple of streams where you dog can get water. The lift gate to the southern end of Low Fell is quite narrow, so the last section of the walk may not be accessible, depending on the size of your dog. There is the possibility of sheep throughout the walk, and from April to July there are ground nesting birds such as skylarks, so it is best to keep your dog under close control and stick to the worn paths.

How to get there – Take the B5292 from Cockermouth to Lorton. Take the B5289 to Low Lorton and then follow the signs for Thackthwaite. The lay-by can be reached on the left, just before the village.

Grid reference – NY 148238
Nearest Postcode – CA13 0RP

Parking – Free in the lay-by

Facilities – There are no facilities

You will need – Dog leads

The Walk

❶ From the lay-by, continue into the village on a slight incline on the quiet road. Pass Brook Farm on your left and, passing the Welcome sign, take the footpath on the right to the side of Thackwaite Farmhouse.

The path is a little rough and ascends, with a garden to your right to begin with. Just as the path becomes wooded your dog will find water from a stream to your left. As you climb a little higher you will have views across the fields to your right.

Put your dogs on leads or under close control before passing through a kissing gate into farmland. Keep to the right of the field, with trees to the field edge. Continue on your ascent. Just before reaching the kissing gate your dogs can find water as it trickles into a trough from a stream. Pass through the kissing gate and continue on your ascent now to the left of the field, beside the stock fence with mature trees, heading towards the stone wall. ❷ Pass through the kissing gate and turn right, with the dilapidated stone wall to your right. You will have views to your right across fields to fells.

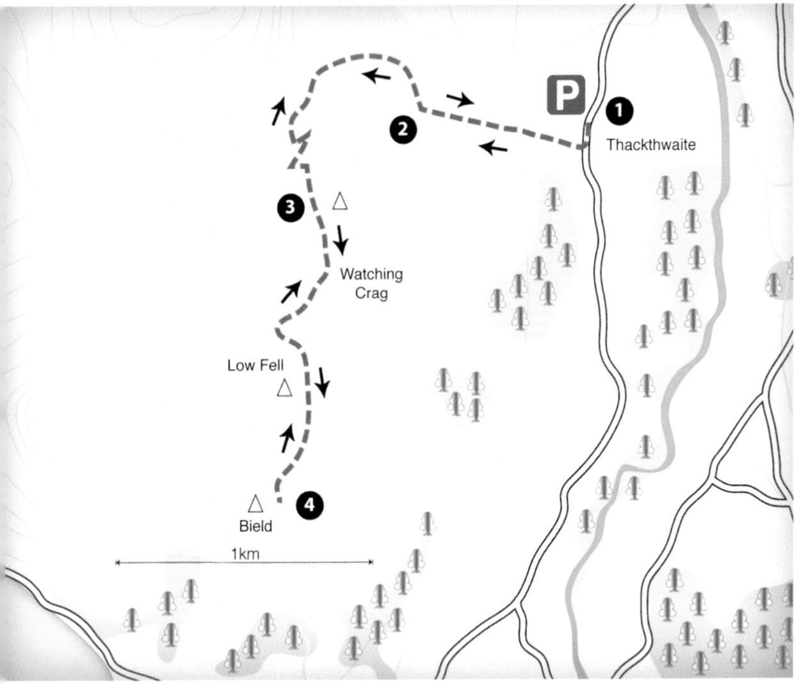

Pass through a gate with a wooded hill ahead of you. The path will bend sharply to the left. Ignore a minor path straight on. Follow the worn, grassy track which cuts into the hillside amongst the fells. The path gets a little steeper, where it bends to the left. Pass through a kissing gate, cutting across the sloped hillside, which is covered in bilberry and some heather.

There is a series of switch-backs to lessen the gradient as you rise toward the fell top. You will get a chance to catch your breath as the path levels out again. Pass through a kissing gate and continue on the worn path. The views are truly spectacular, with fells in all directions and Crummock below. ❸

Continue on the path, with a descent and then an incline once again. Pass over the stile with a lift gate for dogs, followed by a short steep incline, which brings you onto the spine of Low Fell. Once the path levels out, you will be met with stunning panoramic views. When you reach a rock pile you are at the summit.

Continue on the undulating spine of the fell, passing over another stile with quite a narrow lift gate. (This is the last section of the linear walk, so if your dog won't fit through then simply retrace your steps from here). Continue on this path, where you will reach the main summit of Low Fell. ❹ The views now open up to Loweswater on your right with Crummock ahead and to your left. You have reached the furthest point of the walk. Now retrace your steps back to your car.

11. Aira Force

Medium - 2.5 miles - 1.5hrs

This is a delightful walk, starting with the lovely National Trust gardens, following the river, passing through a pinetum and then ascending the gentle slope with some steps to reach the top of Aira Force, a wonderful waterfall. After leaving the garden to enter lovely open grassland amongst the hills and climbing a little, you will be rewarded by the fabulous views over Ullswater and the surrounding hills and mountains. You will pass rocky crags known as Green Hill. There are no roads but there are sheep grazing once you leave the gardens. Your dog will have lots of opportunity for drinks along the way.

How to get there – Take the A592 from Windermere to Penrith on the Kirkstone pass, passing through Glenridding, and immediately after passing the A5091 on the left the car park will be found on the left hand side of the road.

Grid reference – NY 400200
Nearest post code – CA11 0PG

Parking – Pay and display National Trust car park

Facilities – There are toilets in the car park and a tea room

You will need – Dog lead, dog bags

The Walk

❶ From the car park go to the end furthest from the road, and pass through a gateway next to the interpretation panels. Continue on this path passing through a gate, with estate fencing on your right. Continue on the path passing through another gate into woodland.

Pass a stream and then take a path to the left beside a glade, passing through the pinetum. You will soon see a river on your right. Climb the steps and ignore a kissing gate to your left. A stream will pass under the path here where your dog can get water. Ignore a path to the right and then you will begin a descent heading to the bridge. ❷ Put your dog on the lead before approaching the bridge. You can view the top of the waterfall here and there are lovely views from both sides.

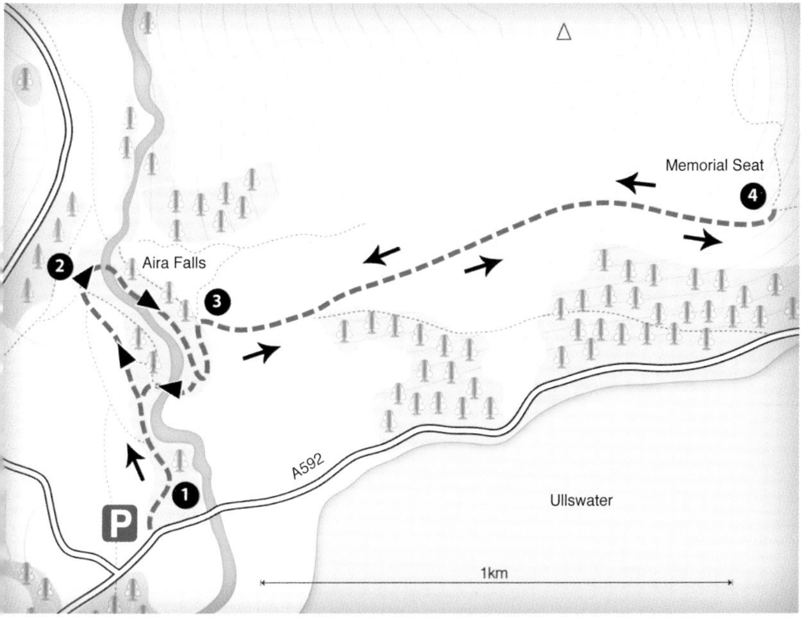

After crossing the bridge ignore the left turn and continue through the gap in the bedrock (veering to the right, not straight ahead). Follow the steps to the lower bridge. When you see the river at the bottom of the steps turn right. Cross over the bridge where you can see the waterfall with its 70ft drop, tumbling between rock faces and surrounded by oaks that are cloaked with mosses and ferns, all adding to the beauty of this magnificent place. Crossing back over the bridge continue on the path, passing the steps on the left. Take the next path on your left, heading back on yourself and ascending the steps. You will have a picket fence to your right and farmland to the other

side. ❸ Where the path forks take the right turn and pass through a gate, ensuring dogs are under close control or on leads at this point as there are sheep grazing. Once reaching another path turn right. You will have views of Ullswater to your right. Stay on the obvious rocky path between the bracken.

When you reach a fork take the left path that ascends the hill, crossing over Hind Crag to the side of Green Hill. There are lots of streams along this path for your dog. As you climb the views are outstanding. You will pass through a scrubby area where the path gets a little rocky, and to your left above you will see the green washed rocky crags known as Green Hill. After climbing a little higher you will reach rocky boulders as the scrub clears.

This is a fantastic spot on a clear day for a picnic looking over Ullswater, the beautiful countryside, woodlands and mountain peaks. The rocks have many lime green lichens that give them a green washed colour from a distance. Continue now on the level section of the path cutting across the slope. After a while another ascent will bring you to another rock crag. You will meet a fence line on your right and then on the left you will see a stone crafted memorial bench that blends in with the area superbly.

Continue a short way on until you have new views ahead of you; this brings you to the furthest point of the walk. ❹ Turn back once you have taken in the views and head back the way you came, down to the main path. Turn right and head back for the National Trust's beautiful garden, entering once more through the small gate.

When you meet another path turn left, descending with some steps, then turn left again descending the steps and cross a bridge. The river is a joy to see, with its hurried clear water that washes over the many boulders. Ascend the steps and turn left on the path staying with the estate fencing. Go through the gate and along the path. When you pass through another gate you will need to put your dog on the lead before reaching the car park once more.

12. Glenridding

Medium - 2.7 miles - 1.5hrs

This walk has tremendous views looking over Ullswater and the Grisedale valley to the mountains beyond, giving you a wonderful alpine feel. There are a few uphill sections but nothing to difficult considering the views you are rewarded with. You will pass through woodland and forest, and alongside rivers and a small tarn with plenty of streams to keep your dog happy. The scenery is absolutely stunning, with open grassland amongst craggy hills and scattered trees surrounded by fells and mountains. There is a quiet access road and sheep on this walk.

How to get there - Take the A592 from Windermere towards Penrith, and once reaching the village of Glenridding you will find the car park on your left off the main road.

Grid reference – NY 385169
Nearest post code – CA11 0PD

Parking – Pay and display

Facilities – There are toilets in the car park and shops and cafes close by.

You will need – Dog leads, dog bags

The Walk

1 From the car park head back to the road, and cross the road bridge over the river turning right to pass the shops and café. Continue along this access road following the river upstream. Once passing the houses you will leave the tarmac onto a dirt road. Ignore the footpath to the right, leaving the river as you begin to ascend on the path. Take the footpath signed Lanty's Tarn, passing a house on the right; just before a second house take the footpath ahead and left. Pass the stunning rocky outcrop with scattered trees, cross a footbridge over a stream where dogs can get water, then on leaving the woods, go through the gate turning right. Keep to the stony path, and then climb the rock steps through the trees.

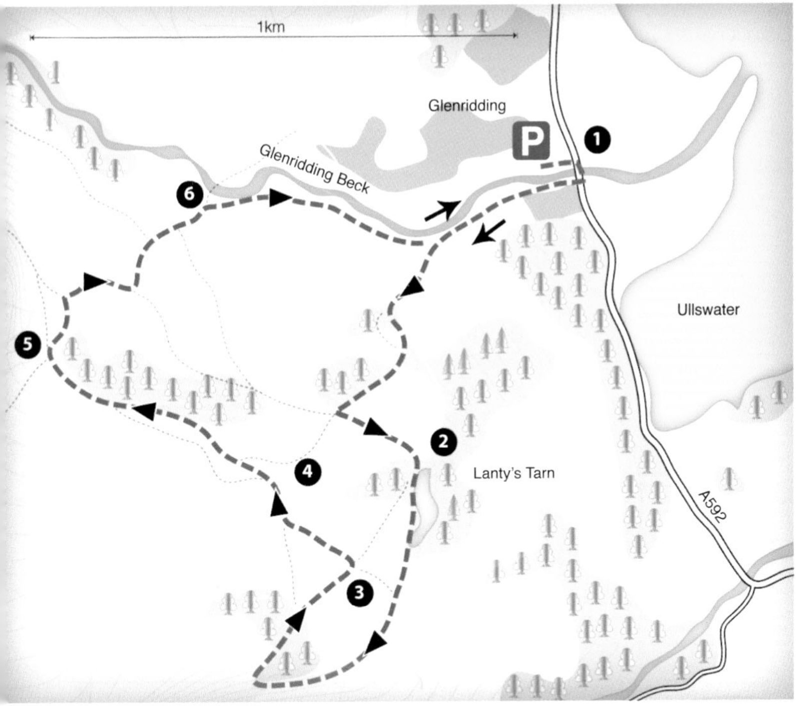

There may be sheep grazing ahead as you pass through a kissing gate to climb a little higher between the bracken hillsides. Once you reach the next kissing gate, look back at the fantastic views of Ullswater and the surrounding countryside and mountains. Turn left once reaching the gate - do not go through it - and continue on your ascent. Have a welcome rest once reaching the plateau, taking advantage of the views before going down towards the forest. **2** Go through the kissing

gate, with the forest on both sides and Lanty's Tarn to your left. Stay on the obvious worn path and as you pass the tarn, ignore a minor path to your right and turn a bend. You will be in awe at the wonderful mountain views that you face as you look down into the Grisedale valley.

Once you meet with another path, turn right following the way marker for Helvellyn. The paths will split; take the path to the right, passing through a gap in the stone wall. When the paths split again, keep with the top path on the right, walking beside the pine trees. Start on another ascent and immediately after reaching the end of the first group of pines take the path on the right, heading up the grassy bank on the worn path with the pines to your right.

Pass through a kissing gate, going through the middle of Brownend plantation and leaving again through another kissing gate. The path is not obvious now for a while. Go straight ahead to pass a rocky outcrop on your right. A little further on turn left and by looking ahead you will see the worn path that ascends towards the stone wall. ❸ Head for this path, veering left, and on reaching the stone wall go through the gate. You will now be in a craggy, rocky area with the most amazing views into the valley, looking over the village and across Ullswater to the mountains and fells that surround it. ❹

Follow on the slightly worn path straight ahead, and when passing close to a rocky crag on your right continue on the path, turning left before the hillside gets too steep. The path will become a little clearer on the opposite side as it levels out. Still you will have amazing views to your right. You will reach a stone wall on your right and crags to your left, where you continue to descend gradually, cutting along the edge of the hillside amongst the stunning mountain scenery.

The path gets a little rocky as you cross the exposed bedrock, and once leaving the stone wall you will reach a more defined stone path. ❺ Turn right on this path, passing over a stream where dogs can get a cooling soak. Turn right again, crossing a smaller stream, and then cross a footbridge. Then turn right passing through the gate. Continue down this path beside the stone wall, enjoying the views as you go. Turn left once you reach another path at the end of the stone wall. You will pass through another gate and follow the path to the road, turning left. Before reaching the road bridge turn right, crossing the stone bridge over the river, and continue on the track, passing a camp site on the right with the river on your left.

You will be walking amongst the trees; once meeting another path turn left, to retrace your steps back to the road and the car park.

13. Grisedale Valley

Medium - 5.7 miles - 3hrs

This walk has wonderful views looking across the valley over Ullswater to the surrounding mountains. You will be surrounded by hills and mountain peaks as you walk amongst rocky boulders and gentle hills in the valley, passing through farmland and peaceful woodland, alongside rivers and streams where you will never be far from the sound of running water and your dogs can get plenty of drinks to cool off. There is a short section of road and sheep on most parts of this walk.

How to get there – Take the A592 from Windermere towards Penrith and once reaching the village of Patterdale, park in the Patterdale Hotel car park on the right hand side of the road just after passing the hotel.

Grid reference – NY 395195
Nearest postcode – CA11 0NN

Parking – Pay and display in the hotel car park

Facilities – There are no facilities

You will need – Dog leads, dog bags

The Walk

1 From the car park, ensuring your dog is on the lead, walk back to the road, cross to the opposite side and turn left. Proceed along the drive of the Patterdale hotel; on reaching the hotel turn right and follow around to the back of the building, turning left and then right to follow the path with a stream alongside it.

The path ascends into the silver birch trees, crossing the stream and then through the gate. You are now in an open area of farmland with sheep grazing so ensure you have close control of your dog. This path inclines gently, passing over and amongst the exposed bedrock between the bracken. You will soon have views over Ullswater to your right as you climb a little higher.

Continue on passing through a kissing gate straight ahead, ignoring the gate on the right just before it. Follow near to the stone wall on the right, keeping to the gravel path. You will have scattered trees on your left and woodland to your right.

Once you pass the woodland on your right you will have stunning views of Ullswater. The path reaches a river where you will need to cross the stepping

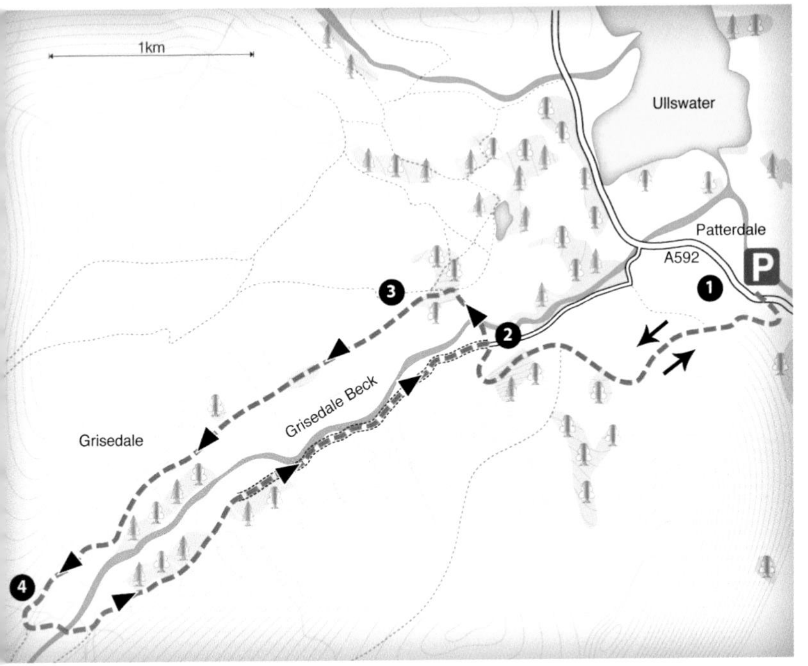

stones. Continue along the path, surrounded by hills and amongst the stunning scenery. There are lots of mountain streams, where your dog will have lots of opportunity to quench his thirst. As you climb a little higher the views are glorious over Ullswater and into the valley. Ignore a path to the left and to the right at the gate, and continue straight ahead with the stock fence and then a stone wall to your right and a forest on the other side.

A little further along you will reach a gate. Ignore this gate and descend a little, crossing a stream. On reaching the sheep fold take the gate on the right, following the obvious path which descends the hill toward the stone barn and passing through a gap in the stone wall. Go through a kissing gate onto a tarmac road, turn right, and then take the kissing gate straight ahead and turn left. Cross the bridge over the river and continue ascending the quiet access road. ❷

As the road bends sharply to the right go through the gate into a field and follow the worn path straight ahead ascending the hill. Go through the gate at the top and turn left. The view is absolutely stunning here looking down into the Grisedale valley and towards the mountains, as glorious as any alpine scene. You will reach a beautiful old iron gate. ❸ Go through the gate and descend on the path following the stone wall on your left. Stay on this path now following into the valley, ignoring a path on the left that heads into the farm on the left. Ignore another path on the left which goes up the hillside at an angle.

You will now be looking into the valley, where there is rough grassland on both sides and enclosed fields at the bottom with lovely stone walls, completely surrounded by hills and mountains. Looking ahead to where the mountains and hills on both sides of the valley meet, this is truly an amazing view, filled with atmosphere. Passing many glacial boulders as you go, you will pass through another gate. Continue to follow the worn path, which will get rocky in places. Pass another gate between stock fencing.

You will cross a bridge over a stream, which looks stunning as it hammers powerfully over the rocks and boulders. Follow the path which meets with a stream and turn left here, crossing the stream just

before you reach the stone sheep fold. If you miss the path you will pass the sheep fold and reach a stone wall and gate. The path will get rocky again here and you will reach another gate. Pass through it and cross the footbridge over the river. There are sheep pens to your left. ❹ It gets a little boggy here so you will need to pick out your path across the rocky area ahead as the path becomes unclear.

On reaching a well worn track turn left and continue, where you will cross a couple of footbridges over streams. You are now walking back along the other side of the valley. The area will become a little enclosed as you reach a stone wall on your left, which encloses woodland. Once past the woodland a lovely large glacial boulder stands in the middle of the field where the stone wall has been built around it. Pass the enclosed fields now on your left and go through another farm gate ahead, passing a stone barn on your right. Then go to the left, continuing with the path. Pass the lovely well made stone walls to your left and woodland on your right. You will pass the farm buildings and farm house on your right.

Continue on this path, which will meet with a river on your left, and pass through a farm gate. Continue straight on with fields to your left and through another farm gate. You will see a stream, which trickles down the rocks on your right and passes under the path to meet the river. The river is lined with trees. Just after passing another mini waterfall to your right you will leave the river behind. There are a few pines to your right in the corner of a field. Follow the stone wall on your right and a little further along ignore a path to the left. You will now be on a sealed path where you continue with the wall.

Pass through another farm gate and continue until you meet back with the kissing gate on your right. Pass back through this and follow the path, passing through the gap in the stone wall and going past the barn on the left. Continue on your ascent on the stony, rocky path, turning left on passing through the gate to retrace your steps back to the car park.

Please keep
dogs under
close control

14. Silver Crag

Medium - 4 miles - 2hrs

This is a beautiful walk amongst stunning scenery, with panoramic views looking over Ullswater and the surrounding hills and mountains. You will pass rocky crags and many rare juniper bushes as you ascend on the steady path cutting across the hillside. A small stream flows down the hillside and weaves its way along to disappear into a cave. There is a short section of road and the possibility of sheep grazing throughout the walk. There are many streams for your dog to get water along the way.

How to get there – Take the A592 from Windermere towards Penrith. Once reaching the village of Patterdale, park in the Patterdale Hotel car park on the right hand side of the road just after passing the hotel.

Grid reference – NY 395195
Nearest post code – CA11 0NN

Parking – Pay and display in the hotel car park

Facilities – There are no facilities in the car park but there is a farmyard tea room near the beginning and end of the walk.

You will need – Dog leads, dog bags

The Walk

❶ From the car park head back onto the road and cross over to make use of the pavement. Turn right and continue until you pass a school and school house on the opposite side of the road. Cross over and take the footpath that passes the school house on your right. Continue along the access track to the farmhouse. Cross a bridge over the river, taking the gate on the right to avoid the cattle grid, and continue on the access track. Walking in the valley, you will be surrounded by hills. Pass through another gate to avoid a cattle grid. Pass houses to your right and a farm building to your left as you proceed through the farmyard, passing a tea shop on your left. Turn right to pass the house on your right and then go through a farm gate.

Continue on the access track, passing a house on the left. Go through another farm gate then turn immediately left to pass through another farm gate. Pass over a sleeper bridge across a stream. The path then bends to the right and then left, ascending the hill. ❷

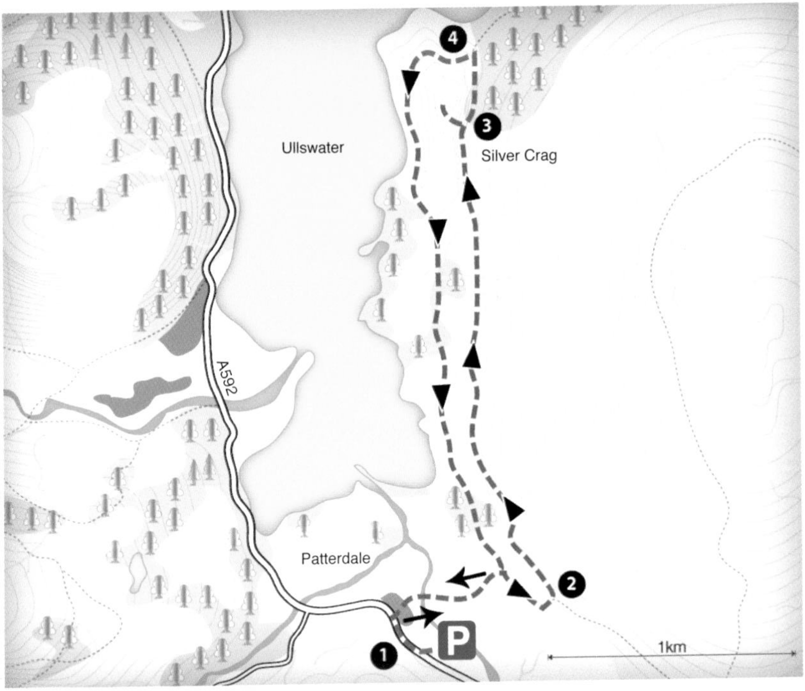

Ignore a right path and continue straight ahead, ascending the hill, with views of Ullswater on the left and ahead as you climb. You will pass slate-like rock faces and lots of scree with scattered hawthorns. You will now have stunning views of the hills and mountains in all directions and rare juniper bushes t the left at the top of the hillside. Where the paths split, take the path on th right that ascends, passing a stream that flows down the hillside twisting a turning over rocks into a cave on your right, a great place for dogs to get a drink. Continue on your ascent, passing a welcome bench where you can sit and take in the fantastic views over Ullswater and the mountains. The path descends a little and then levels out for a while. You will now be walk amongst scattered hawthorns, scree, bracken and craggy rock faces. The path will get a little rocky where it begins to descend again.

Stay on the main worn path, where you will reach the lake and a campsite below you. The hawthorn scrub will thicken a little as you head for Silver C the hill ahead and to your left. You will see Glenridding village on the oppo side of the lake as you continue along the path, passing several welcome streams for your dogs to cool off. You will soon be on a level with the junip bushes as you reach Silver Crag on your left, ascending now on a grassy path. ❸ You can if you wish follow the worn path on your left to the top o the crag to reach the highest point of the walk, walking amongst the junip and rocks that are lime green with lichens. Then turn back down the way came to re-join the path.

Continue past a small pond on your right, then descend on a rocky path w small streams flowing alongside. You will pass the juniper as you go with steps to get you down the steepest sections. ❹ On reaching a path, turn passing another stream as you make your way around the other side of S Crag, now near to the lake. Stay with the main path where, a little further along, you will pass some singular trees as they spread out their branches taking advantage of the space.

Follow on the path as you ascend towards the copse of Scots pine. The p comes near to a stone wall on the right, passing streams as they race dov the hillside. Soon you will be between two stone walls with mixed woodlar your right. The hills to your left will be visible once more as you pass the s wall on your left. Pass a stone building on your right, then ignore a ladder and pass a farm gate. Continue along the path, which will become woode both sides. Ignore a gate on your right just as you pass a stream to your le Continue on, passing through a farm gate. Once through the farm gate int the farmyard, turn right between the farmhouse and farm building, passing welcome tea room where you can have a well-earned rest. Continue along access track and turn left at the road to return to your car.

15. Knott Head

Easy - 1.5miles - 1h

This is a short forest walk, described as easy but there are a few gradual hills. There is a small section of mixed broadleaves, dominated by oak. Your dog can run free without the danger of roads and there is no livestock. You will find lots of water for dogs as gentle streams flow under the network of paths.

How to get there – From Keswick take the A66 signed for Cockermouth. Follow signs for Braithwaite and Lorton on the B5292, which is the Whinlatter pass. Pass through the village of Braithwaite and continue until you reach Noble Knott car park on your left, just as you see a lay-by on the right.

Grid reference – NY 225240
Nearest post code – CA12 5

Parking – Free in the Noble Knott car park

Facilities – There are no facilities except for a picnic bench in the car park

You will need – Dog leads

The Walk

1 From the car park take the footpath ahead of the interpretation board. Take the left path, which ascends through larch at first and has a series of small ascents and descents as it cuts through the hillside.

You will pass some mature oaks with moss covering the bark, amongst the coniferous trees. Another lower path will join the path you are on. Continue straight ahead, ascending. When you meet with another wider track turn left. Your dog will find water as a stream trickles down the hillside and goes under the path. A little further along take the path on your right, **2** which switches back and has an incline.

There are some silver birch and gorse to the edges of the path here, adding a bit of variety within the forest. Take a path on your left. When you see the farm gate and farmland, turn right, following the well-worn path to the edge of the forest, through an open area with some heather, ferns and grasses.

You will pass a stream flowing under the path where dogs can again get water. The path bends sharply to the right. When you meet another path turn right, following a stream on your left. **3** You will reach a wider track; cross this and continue straight ahead, descending into mixed broadleaved woodland which will then become dominated by oak.

Take the narrow path on the right, where you will pass over a couple of quirky planked bridges, made with wood taken from the forest. Ignore a path on your right and continue straight ahead. The path will bend to the right so it is parallel to the road. Take care here, as there are no boundary fences, so you may wish to put your dog on a lead. This path will soon return to the car park.

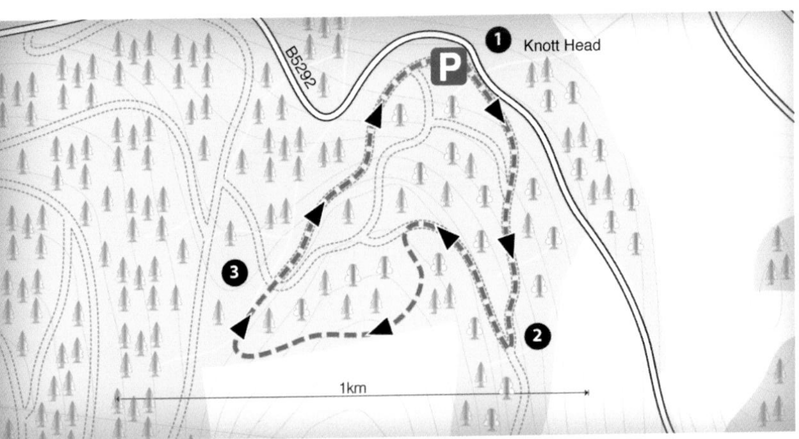

16. Whinlatter

Medium - 3 miles - 2hrs

This is a great forest walk with many shades of green, whatever the time of year. There is a gentle climb for the first half of the walk, but it is well worth the effort as at the top you will have the most amazing views of Keswick and Derwent Water. There is a small section of heathland near to the top, which is glorious when in flower. Your dog will love the freedom and you will be able to relax, as there are no livestock: it is a great place to have relief from the tugging of the lead whilst amongst sheep. There are no roads and your dog will find water along the way.

How to get there - From Keswick take the A66 signed for Cockermouth. Follow signs for Braithwaite and Lorton on the B5292, which is the Whinlatter pass. Pass through the village of Braithwaite and continue until you reach the car park on your right, signed Whinlatter Visitor Centre.

Grid reference – NY 209245
Nearest post code – CA12 5

Parking – Pay and display

Facilities – There are toilets and a café

You will need – Dog leads

The Walk

1 The walk starts from the back of the visitor centre, taking the path to the left which leads to a children's play area. Take the path to the right of the play area following the green way markers.

Take the path ahead and to the right when leaving the play area, passing through the evergreen trees. When you reach a series of benches and an interpretation panel take the second left, heading up a narrow path. The forest is dark here as you pass through the tightly spaced trees.

On reaching a wider forest track turn left and follow the hairpin bend to continue your ascent. There are pockets of heather growing up the banks on either side and the forest floor is carpeted with moss giving colour.

The path levels out here. Follow another hairpin bend to reach an opening on the right with grasses, heather and scattered regenerating trees. On your climb once more you will pass a shale slope on your left.

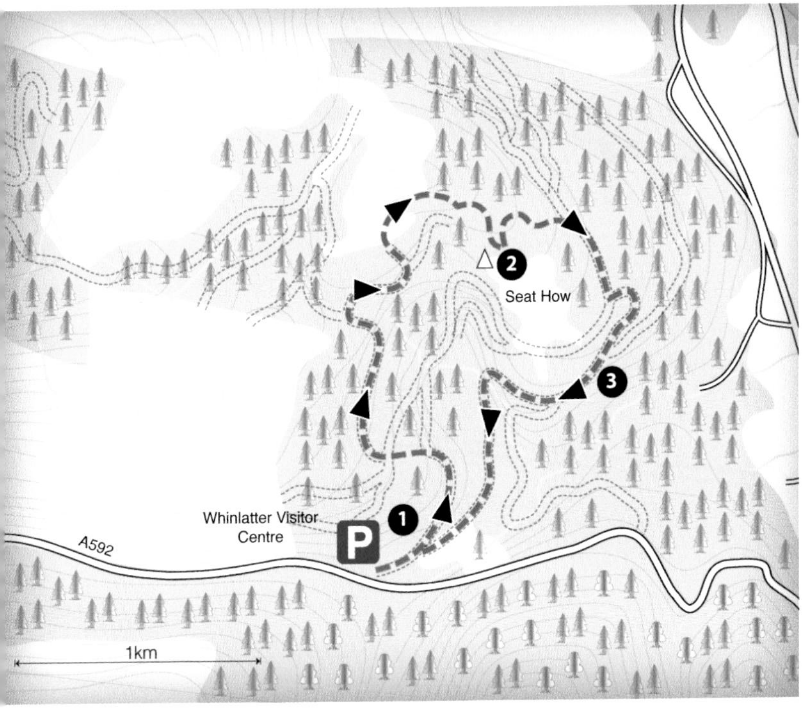

2
Seat How
3
1
Whinlatter Visitor Centre
P
A592
1km

The path narrows as you head back into the trees. When reaching a fork, take the left one, which inclines once more. Look out for a narrow path to the right with a steep ascent to begin with.

As you rise a little higher the area opens out once more. This time it is abundant with heather and bilberries. Stay on the main gravel path; when entering back into the forest your dog will find water as a stream flows under the path.

❷ When you reach another opening surrounded again by heather you will be met with stunning views. Take the path on the left that isn't signed by a green way marker. Here you can sit for a while for the most amazing views over Keswick and Derwent Water, with Bassenthwaite to your left, all framed by mountains and fells.

Now for the descent, return to the path and turn right, where you will wind down the hill until you meet with another wider forest track. Turn right here, passing an exposed rock face to your right and those stunning views again on your left. You will meet another forest track where you turn left, and soon you will see a welcome bench to enjoy those views for the last time. ❸ Continue on the path, passing a path on the right, and follow the hairpin bend. Ignore another path on the right and continue to descend.

You will pass a stream that flows under the path where your dogs can cool off. There are many shades of green here, from the moss-covered ground to the many varieties of coniferous trees. Follow the path on a right hand bend, ignoring the path to the left. You will pass a gate on your left and farmland. Put your dog on the lead here and then pass through a vehicle barrier where you will approach the car park. You will see the visitor centre ahead where you can get a well-earned cup of tea.

17. Loweswater

Challenging - 4.5 miles - 2hrs 30min

This is a stunning walk - you will start level with Loweswater and then climb on a steady journey to gain height, where you will have fabulous views looking over Loweswater and the surrounding fells and mountain peaks. At one of the highest points of the walk there is a bench, making it a great spot for a picnic. There are beautiful woodlands, forest and surrounding countryside with lots of streams to keep your dog happy. There are no roads but you will encounter livestock.

How to get there - From Keswick take the B5292, signed Whinlatter Pass. Then turn onto the B5289 following signs for Loweswater. On reaching the T junction turn left and after passing over a road bridge at Scale Hill take the fourth turning on your left.

Grid reference – NY 134210
Nearest post code – CA13 0RU

Parking – Free in a lay by

Facilities – There are no facilities, but the Kirkstile Inn is close by and is signposted from the road. Dogs are welcome in the bar area until 6pm.

You will need – Dog leads, dog bags

The Walk

❶ From the car park take the gate next to the cattle grid and head along the stone path. Walking in the valley surrounded by hills, you will soon see Loweswater ahead of you.

Pass through a couple of farm gates along this path and then you will be in view of the water's edge. Before reaching a house at the beginning of a small hedge, take the worn path on the right that crosses diagonally right towards a gate.

Once through the gate turn back on the stone track, ignore the path to the left and stay with the lake path through beech dominated woodland. Ignore another path and continue on this well surfaced track. Cross the bridge beside the ford and continue on the main path, which veers left as you pass a stone building, or you could take the path on the right, to walk beside the lake. Both paths will rejoin ahead. You will now be walking in the middle of oak-dominated woodland.

Cross another bridge next to a ford and continue through mixed woodland.

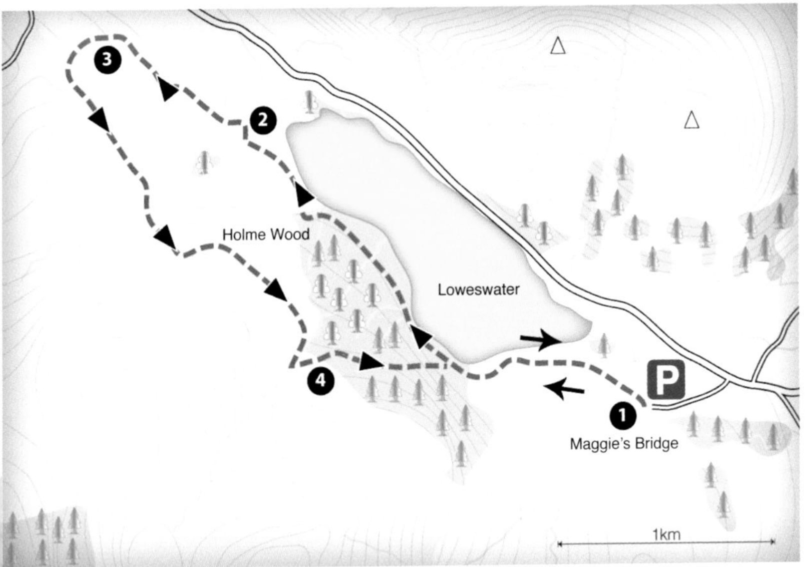

You will pass through another gate, moving out of the woodland, and into open farmland to have lake views once more. Follow an old stone wall on your right, passing through another farm gate where the path begins to incline.

Walking between stock fences surrounded by farmland, pass through another farm gate and turn right passing a farmhouse on the left. ❷ Pass through another farm gate, and passing a couple of houses you then take the gate on the left, keeping the stock fence on the left. Pass through another farm gate, then turn right, keeping the stock fence now on your right. Pass through another farm gate and continue straight ahead, staying with a hedgerow first on your left then on your right. You are now on a steady incline.

Pass through another farm gate and cross the field diagonally left. After passing through another gate you will follow a quiet lane. Look back at the wonderful views. Continue, passing an old water trough on the left then farmhouses and a farmyard on your right. Pass through another gate on a quiet road between farmland. After passing through another gate, before reaching the farmyard and house, take the track to the left which ascends. Pass through another farm gate, staying on the track between the fields with a stone wall on your left. You will have lovely views to your right.

Pass through a sheep fold, and on going through the gate, turn left on to another track. ❸ Follow the stone wall on the left, passing through the large open fields, and go through another farm gate staying on the path. You will have views over the lake to your left. The path will become a little steeper as you gain more height.

Pass through another couple of gates as you continue along this path. On passing through the gate with the ladder stile, turn left to descend down towards the lake far below. There are amazing views here amongst the open farmland, across the water to the hills and mountain peaks all around. The path will descend and ascend. The stunning views will continue, and you will be pleased to see a bench where you can take a well earned rest. This is a great spot for a picnic. Pass over a sleeper bridge and continue on another climb. Take the descending path to the left and then pass through a kissing gate following the worn path descending into the forest. ❹

When reaching a wider track cross this and continue to descend. The forest becomes woodland and you will cross another track to continue descending towards the lake below. Once reaching a wide familiar track, turn right to pass through the gate. Cross the field diagonally left and on reaching the main path continue back to your car.

18. Crummock

Easy - 2.7 miles - 1hr

This walk is absolutely stunning and your dog will love running free in the forest and woods. There are stunning views over Crummock Water to the fells and mountains, and lovely lakeside beaches where you can soak up the atmosphere while your dog enjoys the water. There are no roads but you will cross through some farmland where there are sheep grazing.

How to get there – From Keswick take the B5292 on the Whinlatter pass. Then take the B5289 turning for Loweswater. At the T junction turn left, and a little further on you will see the National Trust car park on your left just before going over a road bridge at Scale Hill.

Grid Reference – NY 149215

Parking – National Trust car park pay and display

Facilities – There are no facilities

You will need – Dog leads, dog bags

The Walk

❶ From the car park go through the gate at the far end into the forest. Ignore a path to the left and continue straight ahead through forest with mixed broadleaved trees. When reaching a fork take the left path.

Ignore a narrow path to your left and continue straight ahead. broadleaved trees known as Lanthwaite Wood soon replace the forest. You will have views to your right over Crummock Water. The path is lined with heather to your left, and as you rise a little higher you will have more views of the lake. The woodlands are delightful with mosses, ferns, heather, bilberry and moss covered rocky boulders here and there. Ignore another narrow path to the left. The path will bend to the left. Just before reaching a gate, turn right on a narrow path, which descends through the woods. You will have a stream to the left and lake views straight ahead.

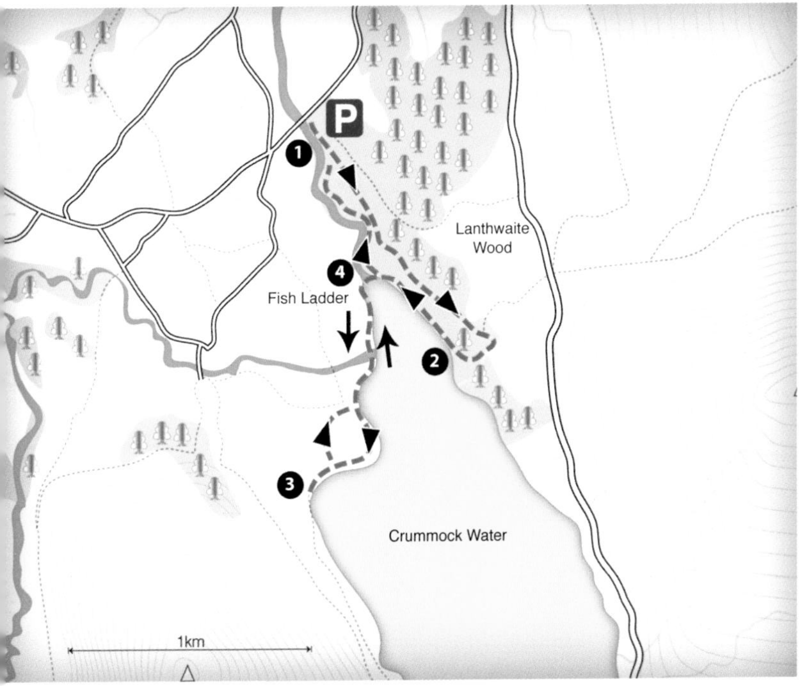

P
1
Lanthwaite
Wood
4
Fish Ladder
2
3
Crummock Water
1km

❷ Once reaching a wider track you can go left to stop for a while at the boathouse where your dog will enjoy the water at the pebble beach, or go right to continue along the track which is lined on both sides with heather. After a little while, take the path on the left, which leads to the water's edge. Your dog will enjoy the water here and you will have beautiful views over the water to the fells. The small fell straight ahead and to the right is Mellbreak, with Red Pike and High Stile beyond.

Now continue along the edge of the water, passing a bench and crossing a suspended footbridge at the weir. Cross another footbridge and follow the path alongside the lake. Pass through the oak trees and then you will come to further beach areas before and after another bridge. You will pass through a gate and a beautiful water tower to your left. Continue on the path, which follows the lake, with a wet grassland meadow to your right.

Pass through a kissing gate into open farmland. You need to ensure that you have good control of your dog as there may be sheep grazing here. Follow the well worn grassy path through a lovely copse of silver birch and hawthorns, with gorse understory, following the pebble path close to the water's edge.

❸ Descend to another great beach where you can have a quiet rest and enjoy the water and the stunning scenery. Now, when you are ready, turn around and head back the way you came, but go up the grassy hill on the other side of the gorse following the well worn path. You will reach a kissing gate. Follow on the familiar path until you have crossed the bridges at the weir. ❹ Once you have crossed the second bridge at the weir take the path on the left which follows alongside the river. Stay on the well-worn path which will eventually return to the car park.

19. Buttermere

Easy - 3.6 miles - 1.5hr

This is a delightful walk around the perimeter of Buttermere, passing next to some lovely woodland with exposed rock faces, boulders and a tunnel that cuts through the rock. You will pass a wonderful waterfall and through forests and farmland. There is a small section of road and there are sheep and cattle grazing. There is water all the way for your dogs.

How to get there – From Keswick take the Honister pass on the B5289 signed to Buttermere. After passing the slate mine and shop on your left, continue along the road until you reach the car park on the left at Gatesgarth farm.

Grid Reference – NY194150
Nearest Post Code – CA13 9XA

Parking – Pay and display from Gatesgarth farm

Facilities – There are no facilities

You will need – Dog leads, dog bags

The Walk

❶ From the car park turn right onto the road and proceed uphill, taking the path that avoids the road for a short while. Once back on the road you will soon see some rocks at the side, on your left. There is a path here that takes you onto a grassy path. Pass through the gorse and over a sleeper bridge, walking beside the rocky outcrops. The road will be above you now.

Pass through a gate; you will be safe from traffic here but there may be sheep grazing so keep your dog under close control.

You will pass some lovely silver birch trees and a gnarly rock crag ahead, which has a bench on the top. Here you can admire the scenery, which is truly stunning in all directions. Continue to follow the lake path, passing a mature ash tree beside the stone wall, and then a copse of Scots pine trees.

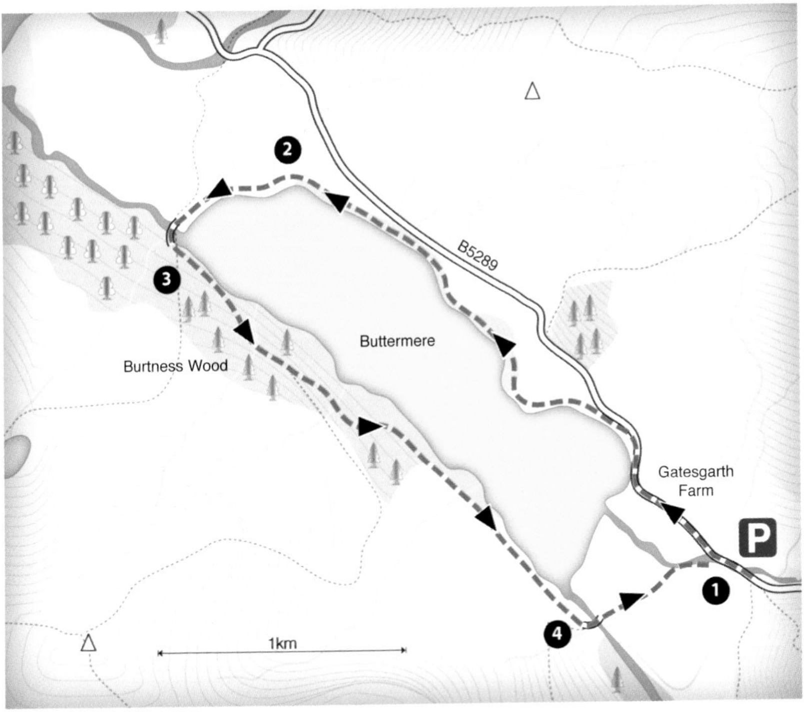

Cross a bridge over a stream, then pass through a kissing gate and turn left. You will see rock crags to the right that

are green with moss. Pass through another gate and climb the rocky section through the mixed woodland, soon following through a tunnel under the rock.

Go through another kissing gate (sheep may be grazing here), following the path into wood pasture with mature trees, cutting across the grazed hillside with gorse and scrub. Pass through another gate into another section of wood pasture then cross another sleeper bridge over a stream.

❷ On reaching a fence line pass through a gate to the left. Turn left again to pass through another gate staying with the water's edge. Follow on this pebble beach, with the fence line to your right and a line of mature sycamore and oak trees to your left. Pass through a gate and stay on the path that follows the water's edge.

❸ Turn right at the end of the path to take the bridge across the river. You will see a waterfall to your right through the oak trees. Cross another smaller bridge and pass through another gate, walking along the edge of the water on your left with woodland to your right. Stay on this path nearest to the lake, where you can enjoy lovely views across the water to the hills and peaks beyond. You will pass some nice lakeside beaches where you can rest for a while and enjoy the water.

Pass through a gap in the stone wall where the woodland is replaced by a forest of larch trees. Where you see three paths you can take the left path or the middle path as they both meet up ahead. The left path is quite narrow in places but stays close to the water. If you have taken the left path you will meet the middle path again shortly, turning left onto it. Pass through a gate into open countryside

with panoramic views of lovely mountain crags and buttresses. There may be Highland cattle here. They are usually of a gentle nature and are well used to people and dogs, so they shouldn't give you any trouble. If you think there is a risk that your dog will chase the cows ensure you have him on a lead or under close control.

Keeping with the raised stoned path, you will join with a stone wall on your left for a short spell. Cross a bridge over a stream. To your left you can see the water flowing off the hillside, with a number of small waterfalls.

You will meet with another stone wall where you stay with the lower path, now nearing the end of the lake. Go left, passing through a kissing gate and then straight ahead between the stock fences. Cross the bridge over the river and pass between the farmland, with a hedge to your left. ❹

Pass through another kissing gate where you need to keep to the edge of the field. You will meet with a river on your left; continue on towards the farm buildings, staying on the path. Pass through a gate on the left of the farmyard and follow the path. On reaching the stock fence turn right between the river and the farmyard. Once you reach the road you will see the car park.

20. Ennerdale

Easy - 2 miles - 1hr

This is a fantastic short walk; it has lakeside paths with views of the surrounding mountains, forest and beautiful broadleaved woodland, which has a small but wonderful waterfall, and your dog will find lots of water from streams and Ennerdale Water. There may be sheep grazing and there is a quiet access road.

How to get there – From Cockermouth take the A5086 signed Egremont. When you reach Lamplugh follow signs for Ennerdale Bridge. Then follow for Croasdale and Ennerdale Water.

Grid reference – NY 110153
Nearest post code – CA23 3

Parking – Free in the Bowness Knott car park

Facilities – There are no facilities on this walk

You will need – Dog leads, dog bags

The Walk

❶ From the car park, head to the furthest end from the road. Take the path to the right onto a sealed track and turn left. You will now have lovely views of the lake.

Continue on this access road with the forest on your left. The road changes from tarmac to stone and you will soon be beside the lake. Pass a wooded finger of land that reaches into the water. You can sit here for a while on the picnic benches and let your dog enjoy the water's edge. Continuing on the path, you will pass willow, silver birch and larch to your left.

❷ Take the next path on the left into mixed woodland. The path will ascend a little as you go. There are lots of woodland flowers here with honeysuckle growing up along the young trees. There are lots of bilberry, mosses and rocky boulders, Scots pine and young oak and holly. Continue through the woodland, which becomes mainly Scots pine to your left and larch to your right. Walk a little further, passing again through mixed woodland with lots of bilberry on the woodland floor.

You will reach a footbridge crossing over a stream, known as Dry Beck. The path will descend now through the forest with heather to the edge of the path. Take a path to the left but don't cross the footbridge over Smithy Beck. You can view a lovely small waterfall here, with ferns and gorse amongst rocky boulders. Then cross back over the bridge reaching the path once more, turning left and walking with the river to your left. ❸ Continue on this path through the mixed deciduous woodland. You will reach a wider stone track, where you turn right following with the lakeside to your left. ❹ There are little beach areas where you and your dog can enjoy the water. Stay on this path now until you reach the car park.

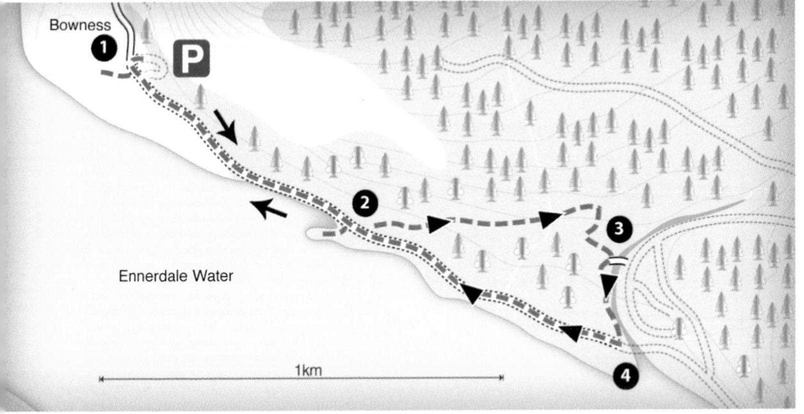

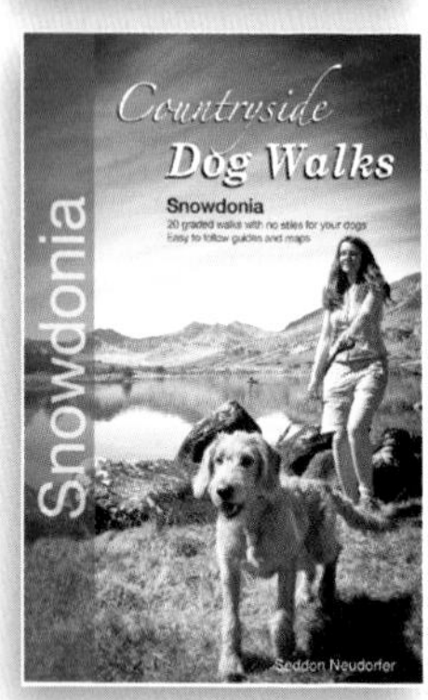

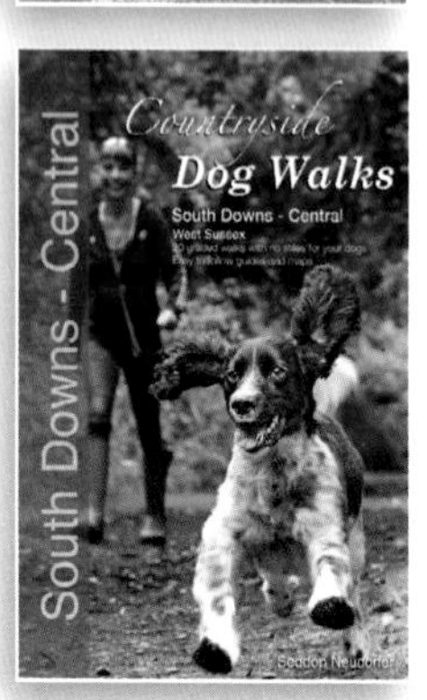

Follow us on Facebook for progress reports on our future publications.

Search - Countryside Dog Walks